Praise for *Getting the Second Appointment*

"Another great book from Tony Parinello! If you've ever lost a sale between your initial presentation and the second visit, this book is for you! Learn how to keep more of the sales you thought you made."

> —Tom Hopkins, sales trainer and
> author of *How to Master the Art
> of Selling*

"Finally, here is a powerful, practiced, no-nonsense book that tells you exactly what to do and say to make more sales faster. A masterpiece!"

> —Brian Tracy, author of *Goals*

"Tony Parinello's new book, *Getting the Second Appointment*, is terrific. It is jam packed with solid sales strategies and tactical tips that will improve any sales professional's top line!"

> —Don Hutson, CEO, U.S. Learning
> and author of *The Sale*

"This is Tony at his best—non-stop and high value."

> —Dave Stein, author of *How
> Winners Sell*

"Tony's style and approach has made him one of the most popular speakers, radio hosts, and authors. Through his book he teaches the salesperson what to ask, say, and when to say it to get the second appointment and effectively perform the two-call close."

> —Dave Mattson, vice president of
> sales, Sandler Sales Institute

"Tony Parinello has done it again! Another original book full of practical examples, useful step-by-step strategies, and compelling insights to help salespeople be more successful. The e-learning exercises that provide the reader with simulated practice opportunities and the author's holistic approach help make this book stand out as no other does."

—Madelyn Burley-Allen, president,
Dynamics of Human Behavior

"If you need bigger sales in the shortest possible time while getting customers to love and trust you for life, then Tony Parinello is the only author who can guarantee you will reach your goals. Tony changed my life and remains the foundation of my success."

—Nance Rosen, author of *Why Customers Buy*

"After reading *Getting the Second Appointment,* I'm convinced that if I had had this information when I started my business in 1987 we would be hundreds of thousands of dollars richer today. This book should be in the library of every entrepreneur."

—Susan Berkley, president, The Great Voice Company, Inc. and author of *Speak to Influence: How to Unlock the Hidden Power of Your Voice*

"A killer guide to sales success—A karate chop to every sales barrier you've ever encountered."

—Peter Montoya, author of *The Brand Called You* and publisher of *Personal Branding* magazine

Getting the
SECOND APPOINTMENT

Getting the
SECOND
APPOINTMENT

How to CLOSE Any Sale in Two Calls!

ANTHONY PARINELLO

WILEY

JOHN WILEY & SONS, INC.

Published by John Wiley & Sons, Inc., Hoboken, New Jersey.
Published simultaneously in Canada.

For general information on our other products and services please contact our Customer Care Department within the United States at (800) 762-2974, outside the United States at (317) 572-3993 or fax (317) 572-4002.

Wiley also publishes its books in a variety of electronic formats. Some content that appears in print may not be available in electronic books. For more information about Wiley products, visit our web site at www.wiley.com.

Library of Congress Cataloging-in-Publication Data:

Parinello, Anthony.
   Getting the second appointment: how to close any sale in two calls! / Anthony Parinello.
        p.   cm.
   Published simultaneously in U.S. and Canada.
   ISBN 0-471-48723-6 (pbk. : alk. paper)
   1. Selling.   I. Title.
HF5438.25. P3613   2004
658.85—dc22

                                                           2003021761

Printed in the United States of America.

10   9   8   7   6   5   4   3   2   1

In Memory of
Catherine E. Jones
Thank you for your dedication to my work.
Thank you for your Friendship . . .
"Bye Sweetie"

CONTENTS

PREFACE

When you get initial face-to-face meetings with prospects, do they seem interested at first . . . and then begin to "stall" when it comes time to move forward in the relationship?

Do you find yourself struggling to get the appointment after you've had what felt like a "superb" initial phone discussion with a prospect?

Have you ever had the unfortunate experience of losing a really good prospect or customer to your competition . . . following a mysterious silence in the relationship?

If you answered, "yes" to any of these questions . . . welcome to the job of selling in the New World Economy.

In this economy, the cost of selling products, services, and solutions continues to rise; the integrity of unique value selling propositions has been severely affected by technology, which has also driven competitive price points to an all-time low; and accurate sales forecasting seems all but impossible.

This unfortunate combination has fueled the erosion of margins and shareholder value in large and small enterprises alike. American businesses—and the people who sell for them—are searching to find New World Marketing and Selling techniques that will help quickly turn rising costs into rising revenues.

How can we revamp today's sales process so that we *thrive*, rather than just survive?

Answer: By getting more quality second and subsequent appointments with the right people.

TURNING IT AROUND

We live in a world where the salesperson with the most unique, memorable, and immediately valuable selling proposition often wins the commitment. It is now critically important to *quickly* turn a "suspect" into a "prospect" and a "prospect" into a lifetime "customer."

In other words, *time-to-revenue* is now a critical measurement of sales success. As a result, the ability to set second and subsequent meetings *with the right players* has never been more important.

That is the skill that will help you turn your business around in the New World Economy. And that's the skill this book will give you.

MY PROMISE TO YOU

I'm a salesperson, just like you. I want to be led, not pushed; I want to be coached, not intimidated. I want to learn from someone who is still in the game. When I have a difficult sales situation, I want to get sound advice from someone who is in the know . . . someone who will *show* me how, not just *tell* me how . . . someone who will show me what works.

And that's the kind of guidance you're going to find in this book.

AND SPEAKING OF COACHING

I've had the fortunate experience in the past year and a half to have a professional success coach helping me focus on my goals (like writing this book) and keeping me personally accountable to achieve my plans and keep my commitments. Why do I need someone like that? Because everyone who wants to reach mastery (in this lifetime) in their profession does. Not everyone is willing to admit it. But, statistics have proven that if you take two individuals of equal skill and provide them with equal opportunity, the one with a personal success coach will perform best. Simple and true; in the sports world and in the world of sales, *coaching* works. The really great news is that I have asked my personal success coach, Steve

Dailey, to coach you! At the end of several really tough chapters in this book, you'll have a chance to meet Steve up close and personal and benefit from his techniques and wisdom. It's all here; it's all for you; all you have to do is turn to the first chapter.

Here's to your future!

P.S. Oh, one other thing, at the end of several chapters of this book, you will be invited to access online assets—downloadable information with new articles and updates that will help you schedule more second and subsequent appointments . . . and close more sales. Take advantage of this online resource—and keep in touch!

FROM COACH STEVE

As you read this book, you have the opportunity to use it one of two ways:

1. As a form of entertainment.
2. To prepare for Peak Sales Performance.

Look back on anything you have ever accomplished in life—those things that you are most proud of. I think you will find a common denominator in one simple truth: *You took action.* You didn't watch passively, You weren't a spectator, you didn't sit around observing someone else . . . *you were in the game.* Those moments in life when you were a hero, reached the mountaintop, or rang the bell all had one thing in common: You were right in the middle of the experience, offering all your heart, soul, blood, sweat, and courage.

If you sincerely picked up this book to become a better salesperson—or to train others to be better salespeople—then you must also be determined to *ACT!*

Throughout the book, Tony will recommend that you write things down, fill in blanks, go to a web site, think about your habits, and challenge your old practices. Meanwhile, I will show up periodically as your coach. My job is to reinforce Tony's principles, challenge you to internalize and practice Tony's principles, and guide you through the Critical Sales Success Steps.

(continued)

As you come upon the exercises and assignments—*Do Them. Take Action! Get in the Game!*

This approach is not only critical to the value that you receive from this book. It is critical to the way you function as a *sales professional.*

If you are not currently performing at your optimum potential, there is a reason. Could it be that you have developed a resistance to trying new ideas or skills? Could it be that you think that you "already *know* how to sell"? Or is it that you look at fundamental principles, practices, or exercises as "only for the rookie"? In any of these cases— or if there's any other reason you can come up with—new levels of performance will require new ways of thinking and an open mind to develop new habits.

This is your chance. Get in the game. ACT! Dive in to the rich, powerful wisdom that Tony offers through experiencing the exercises and act on the challenges we each make of you. Your future success depends on it.

MEET STEVE DAILEY

Your next best friend and your competition's nemesis. During the past twenty-five years Steve has been a success coach for hundreds of business professionals. He's no armchair strategist; he started his first business with less than $200 and shaped it into a multimillion-dollar organization in just three years! Coach Steve is the founder of Prime Focus Inc., a coaching and consulting enterprise that serves entrepreneurs, business executives, and sales professionals in a multitude of business models and marketplaces. You'll learn more than one life changing idea from his teachings and you'll come to know Coach Steve as one of your greatest raving fans. His unconditional support and dedication to your personal achievement are simply . . . epic. You can contact Steve directly at: sdailey@primefocuscoaching.com.

ACKNOWLEDGMENTS

A hardy thank you is in order for the following individuals: To my over one million alumni, my many customers, and to my personal success coach Steve Dailey. A very special thanks to my dear friend and mentor Denis Waitley for introducing me to the wonderful folks at John Wiley & Sons, Inc. They are simply the most professional, helpful, and friendly publishers on this planet. And to you, my new friend, thank you for reading this book. I look forward to getting to know you.

Finally, to all of my Guardian Angels who keep opening doors ahead of me. Josephine Rose, my mother; Al, my brother; and Catherine E. Jones, my greatest raving fan.

A. P.

INTRODUCTION

The idea for this book came to me one day as I sat waiting for the telephone to ring. Oh, I wasn't just sitting doing nothing, I was looking at the words on my computer screen that I had typed in the "notes" field of my contact manager that read: "proposal accepted, budget approved, contract to be signed by next Tuesday 9/15" my eyes scanned what followed, a series of other less descriptive entries: "9/16 VM WCB," "9/19 VM WCB," "9/20 VM WCB" by the way "VM" is my code for leaving a Voice Mail message and "WCB" means that the prospect will call back. But *this* prospect never did. The list of VM WCBs is too long to repeat here. The date was December 2 and I still was waiting. I began scanning the "notes" field of a multitude of other prospects that all had their fair share of VM WCB codes. Each of these prospects was interested initially and somewhere between the first appointment and the proposal their interest wandered off. Now, I sat silently in this place that over the past 28 years I have come to call "sales hell."

This book is about avoiding the waiting game and avoiding sales hell. This book is about being so good at selling that you'll attract natural customers who will buy from you and they'll do so on the second appointment. I can just hear you saying, "Wait a minute, Tony. It 'typically' takes me six months to a year to sell." I wouldn't argue with you. I am sure it does take that long for you to sell. I contend that most every prospect in the world knows if they're going to "buy" from you long before you "sell" them anything. And, yes, in this book, you'll learn how to make the sale on the second appointment . . . or walk from the deal.

Before you put this book back on the shelf and walk away shaking your head saying "that guy was nuts. What a crazy idea . . . sell *my* product in two calls, what does he know?"

HERE'S WHAT I KNOW

In the past 15 years, I have taught well over one million salespeople and the majority of the Fortune 500 how to get appointments with top officers by using the tactics that I have developed and published in my best-selling book: *Selling to VITO*™ the Very Important Top Officer. Now, I've focused my 28 years of sales experience and the best-practices advice from my alumni on the topic of "Getting the Second Appointment" to create the book you are now holding in your hands.

Don't put it down. Instead, let's turn the page . . . together.

1

SUCCESS AND YOUR SALES CAREER

Most books on sales *end* with a chapter on success. This book *begins* with one.

Typically, authors of books on selling assume that by the end of the book the reader will have all the tools and will be ready to push the "launch" button, get the desired result, and become the winner he or she was born to be. In putting this book together, I realized a different approach was in order.

After personally training more than one million salespeople and coaching many more on my Internet radio talk show, I can say without any hesitation that most salespeople come to books, tapes, and other resources *already* in possession of at least some of the tools they need . . . and are *already* sitting on top of what is known in the trade as a "performance plateau." In other words, they've got a problem exceeding their known or perceived limits.

Translation: No matter how high or low their performance plateau may be, most salespeople do have such a plateau. They get just a little too comfortable with where they are. And they stagnate.

This book is about breaking up that stagnation by getting more second appointments.

This book is about specific skills that will help you schedule a higher percentage of second meetings with the people you meet for the first time.

This book is, in other words, about strategies for *changing* what you're doing right now.

As a matter of personal experience, I can assure you that changing what you're already doing is not always easy. But bringing about change is essential if you plan to break through your personal performance plateau—wherever it may be.

To implement meaningful change, people must first overcome what I call the "complacency challenge." And that's why this book begins, rather than ends, with a chapter about success and what it means to you.

THE COMPLACENCY CHALLENGE

If I am going to ask you to change the way you're selling, or to change the expectations and the results that you get from your sales efforts, then I must first give you some strategies for overcoming the challenge of being comfortable right where you are. Otherwise, you will (alas) be statistically unlikely to implement the ideas for generating more second and subsequent appointments that appear in the later chapters. As a practical matter, we have to address the complacency challenge before we address the second-appointment challenge. If you doubt this, consider the sobering fact that studies have shown that *fewer than 10 percent* of all people who buy books designed to help them improve their life or career ever finish reading the book!

If you're motivated enough to have picked up this book and started reading, we've already got a little bit of traction on overcoming complacency. Now I want to challenge you to make the most of that momentum by taking a few moments with me to examine where you are in your sales career right now, and where you would like that career to take you.

A WORD ABOUT SELF-SABOTAGE

Self-sabotage is a fancy term for having a fear of success. Many salespeople suffer from this problem without even realizing it. It's one of the big reasons that people experience career plateaus in sales.

I consider myself an expert in the field of identifying and battling *success phobia*—because I myself am a recovering success phobic.

The truth is, I have literally "failed my way to success." What do I mean by that? I mean that I made some big mistakes in my selling career, mistakes that I was able to turn around by reprogramming some very dangerous negative thinking patterns. These were damaging, self-perpetuating internal mental patterns, patterns that I eventually realized reflected a fear of achieving above a certain level in my career. Thank goodness I was able to get over them! If you're like most salespeople, you've got some negative thinking patterns to address, just as I did.

Why would anyone be fearful of sales success? There are many reasons, perhaps as many different reasons as there are people who become salespeople. What's more important than the *why* is the *how*. We become fearful of success as a result of the things we say to ourselves . . . without using our mouths. If you think of the brain as a tape recorder, and monitor what it "plays" on a regular basis, you may realize that it's sending you messages like the following:

- "Why would this person want to meet with *me* again?"
- "Sure, I closed the sale, but one thing's for certain—good times never last."
- "It seems like a good opportunity, but there's got to be a catch. There's no free lunch."
- "That was pure, dumb luck."
- "I should be thankful for what I have—life could be a whole lot worse."
- "A bird in the hand is worth two in the bush."
- "This is too easy."
- "What makes me think I'm so good?"
- "That person/department/organization—is working harder than I am. They probably deserve this deal more than I do."
- "Anything that can go wrong, will go wrong."

Those are just a few of the examples of negative self-talk that I've helped people (including myself) to turn around over the years.

Just so you know what you're likely to be up against . . . why not take a moment and write down at least four "self-sabotage" messages your brain might play automatically when the time comes to set a second or subsequent appointment and get the sale.

Once you can recognize negative self-talk, you'll find that it's much easier to replace it with positive self-talk. For instance:

- "I know I can help this person."
- "People who decide to meet with me for a second time are glad they did."
- "I'm the sort of person who can make the best of any situation."

Now write down at least four positive self-talk messages you can say to yourself when you set a second or subsequent appointment and get the sale.

TO THE IMPORTANCE OF OVERCOMING
SUCCESS PHOBIAS

As you will learn, setting more second and subsequent appointments is nothing more—or less—than mastering a series of sales skills. It's something you can learn, practice, and develop expertise in. Like many such skills, though, to implement them on a consistent basis, you must prepare yourself psychologically for the positive results you are likely to bring about in your life.

Translation: If you're still stuck in a self-sabotage mode, what you're about to learn in the chapters of this book won't do you much good.

There are some psychologists who will tell you (for a hefty price) that the fear of success is the result of low self-esteem or a lack of self-confidence. Actually, that's just the tip of the iceberg. My experience in breaking through self-imposed limitations suggests that

fear of success starts when we embrace a set of negative precon-
ceived notions—ideas that can be called *disempowering beliefs.*

These beliefs are the ideological principles that
make negative self-talk possible. They tend to be
short, universal-sounding statements. They may
sound like this:

- "Life is tough."
- "Only the strong survive."
- "Success is difficult to achieve, and it's only
  for the gifted."
- "Some people have all the luck."
- "I was born on the wrong side of the tracks."
- "Look what my parents did to me."

> Removing
> negative self-
> talk is easy.
> Start by
> deleting the
> "apostrophe"
> and the letter
> "t" from the
> phrase "I can't."

The principle that it's nearly impossible to attain
success is so deeply ingrained in our thinking that
when we *don't* encounter insurmountable situations,
when success without undue hardship *does* come into sight, we instinctively sabotage our own efforts, play those negative messages
on our mental tape recorder, and stop short of realizing our dreams.

TAKE A DEEP BREATH . . .

To start moving past your personal success plateau, begin by taking the first of a series of deep breaths . . . and giving *honest* answers to each of the following questions:

1. Are you finding fewer *new* customers now than you did
   when you first started selling at your current job?
2. Is your base of existing customers and the amount of business you get from them "flat"—or growing more slowly
   than it once did?
3. Does everything in your sales process seem to take longer
   than it used to?
4. Do you find that you're slower than you used to be on following up on new leads or referrals that you receive?
5. Do you feel less happy or fulfilled than you were when you
   started out as a salesperson?

6. Have you stopped doing something that once worked well in your sales efforts?
7. Is your lifestyle and general quality of life of a higher quality than it was when you were growing up
8. Is your income currently more than that of your parents? (After you adjust it for inflation.)

(Keep taking deep breaths—we're almost done.)

9. Do you have the overall feeling that life in general, and your career specifically, could be better?
10. When you finally do reach a goal that you wanted, do you feel that you no longer want it as much?
11. Do your accomplishments come only when there is a deadline?
12. Do you downplay and downgrade your accomplishments when someone offers you praise?
13. Do you feel any sense of guilt when you achieve a level of performance that's higher than your peers?

CHANGE THE MESSAGE, CHANGE THE RESULTS!

If you answered "yes" to any one of these questions, you are probably sending your brain *mixed messages* about your professional objectives. Part of you is picking up the phone and getting ready for meetings . . . part of you is holding back and undercutting your own sales achievement.

Mixed messages get in the way of the goal of setting more second appointments with prospects. In fact, mixed messages get in the way of the larger goal of success as a salesperson!

For all but a few of us who have chosen a career in sales, the reason we send these mixed messages has to do with our early years and our upbringing. The simple fact is that most of our parents are or were middle class or lower–middle class, and as such had certain levels of economic and social stature. Generally speaking, when we experience life that is well within these levels we feel quite comfortable.

As we progress in life, we eventually reach a point in our careers where we find that, the further away we get from these preprogrammed economic and social stature positions, the more pronounced our discomfort becomes. In extreme cases, we actually begin to back down and away from success until we unintentionally sabotage our future success . . . so that we stay within (or at least in close proximity of) our past comfort levels. The tape that's playing inside our heads plays the necessary messages louder and louder. "Be careful . . . you could lose it all!" "What makes you think you're so good?" "Be happy with what you have!" and so on.

This chapter will help you see where you are in relation to those messages and empower you to make a *choice* as to where you want to be and allowing yourself to achieve that level rather than any preprogrammed level.

MASTERING THE PROCESS—AND GETTING THE APPOINTMENT!

Consistently getting a second or subsequent appointment, like any other result, is a process. We can implement that process and get good results—once we turn off any other, unproductive processes that may be in operation. Fortunately, that's not too hard. With relative ease, we can totally change our self-limiting message to a self-empowering message.

Throughout this book, I provide success messages and assignments for you to use to overcome most or all of the self-limiting thoughts and beliefs that may undercut your self-confidence, your desire to achieve, and your ability to set second appointments or other meetings with sales prospects. Take advantage of these exercises . . . starting right now!

HERE'S OUR STARTING POINT

Believe it or not, our prospects and customers have similar fears and insecurities when we make attempts to sell to them. (You'll find out much more about this phenomenon in later chapters.) So think about that for a minute. Here we sit with our own self-limiting messages, and we're trying to convince people to meet with us who have a set of negative messages all their own.

Why *shouldn't* our prospects feel insecure? We salespeople ask them to invest in products, services, and solutions that cost

> Getting the second appointment and making the sale in two calls requires a skill set that can be learned.

more than a month, year, or lifetime of their salary . . . and then we send them *our* fear and insecurity signals (subtly or overtly), so they get the message "I don't really believe in what I'm doing or in my own ability to succeed!" Then we wonder why they don't want to see us again or buy from us.

What I am about to share with you will change the way you think and sell. It's an easy six-step process that, when followed, will free you from the self-limiting indecision that reinforces the fears and insecurities of our prospects, and holds our own careers in place.

It's time for another deep breath; get plenty of oxygen to your brain. Ready?

Step One

Ask: "What is happening right now in my career that is limiting my performance or causing a problem?"

Possible Responses:
- Call reluctance (will think of any reason not to pick up the phone).
- Unwilling to try new techniques and tactics.
- Empty sales funnel.
- Prolonged slump.
- Heavy competitive pressures.
- All the other possible responses.

Write *your* answer(s) here:

_____

_____

_____

_____

_____

Step Two

Ask: "How is this situation making me feel?"

It's best to be very specific about the actual feeling(s) that you are experiencing. Ask yourself the simple but very powerful question: "When I experience (the competition stealing my customers) how does that make me feel?"

Note: Basically, there are only four feelings—Happy, Sad, Angry, Scared—each with its specific qualifiers.

Possible Responses:

- Angry: It's costing me customers and market share.
- Sad: I am below quota again this month.
- Scared: If it continues I'll be on probation.

Write *your* answer(s) here:

_____

_____

_____

_____

_____

Step Three

Proceed immediately by asking yourself: "What is this costing me?"

This answer can be articulated by using a dollar amount or by descriptive words and phrases.

Possible Responses:

- Angry: "Three sales this month alone that's $325,000 in revenue and $6,000 in commission checks."
- Scared: "My attitude is in the tank. I am totally embarrassed at each sales meeting when I've got to 'fess up to the fact that I am losing customers to the competition."

Write down your feelings and what your self-imposed limitation(s) are costing:

_____

_____

_____

_____

Step Four

This is the tricky one: You must identify what resources are available now that you can use to resolve this situation.

Is there another salesperson in your organization who is an expert in beating the competition? If there's a sale that you just lost, can you call the prospect and ask some pointed questions as to why they selected the competition and not you? Does your marketing department have any information that you could use to better prepare yourself for the next attack from your competition? Is there some way that you can find out about the competition's products and their approach to selling? Can you find out something specific about the competitor's salesperson that is costing you customers?

There are plenty of places to look for information that could help you turn the situation around. Take a moment now and write down a minimum of 10 resources available to you for possible solutions. Don't stop until you've got all 10, and keep breathing nice and deep.

1. _____

2. _____

3. _____

4. _____

5. _____

6. _____

7. _____

8. _____

9. _____

10. _____

Step Five

Now—look at this list and select the single most *difficult* item to accomplish. Next, select the three actions that would be the *easiest* for you to accomplish. Finally, organize the remaining six in order of difficulty, with the least difficult first.

Step Six

Make a personal commitment to tackle the easiest three action items within the next five business days.

Make a personal commitment to tackle the six action items you prioritized at some point in the next 15 business days following that.

Finally, agree to tackle the most difficult item on the twenty-first business day.

KEEP YOUR COMMITMENTS

The process that you just completed has been used by professional sports and business coaches and has been refined, tested, and proven over the years on many top performers. This process will help you build your *personal accountability*—and will help you send confidence signals to customers and prospects that make it very easy for them to continue a business relationship with you. Here, and in the chapters that follow, Coach Steve Daily will serve as your personal success coach. That means he will challenge you to follow through on what you've learned . . . and to keep your commitments to yourself. It's our job to help you get to the top of your mountain . . . so that when you get there, you can coach someone else to the top.

With the purchase of this book, you have been given a free trial period to embrace my second *Appointment Success Portal*. To start your membership, go to: www.gettingthesecondappointment.com and click on: Success Portal.

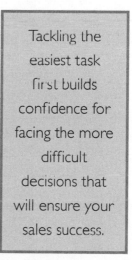

Tackling the easiest task first builds confidence for facing the more difficult decisions that will ensure your sales success.

FROM COACH STEVE

Let's talk in a little more depth about *self-sabotage.*

Another phrase for self-sabotage is "failure avoidance." Yet, failure avoidance sounds, at first, like a reasonable objective. Many of us view failure as a negative experience and therefore (consciously or unconsciously) attempt to avoid it.

But let me appeal to your logic for a moment: When did you ever accomplish anything in life that was truly significant, without failing in your first—or even many subsequent—attempts?

Failure is *not* the opposite of success. Failure is, necessarily, *part* of any meaningful success we achieve in life.

If you attempt to achieve anything in life that is new, more, different, better, then you also necessarily will have experiences that you have never had before. It is completely unreasonable to expect yourself to execute anything perfectly in your first attempt. Even if you could, you would likely wonder if it was luck the first time. Let go of the unrealistic, self-limiting belief that failure is a bad thing. Failure is a part of any victory. Without the abrupt feedback of failures, you would not learn. Without the contrast of failure, you would not recognize victory. Without the experience of failure, there would be no wisdom.

Read Tony's stories. He is one of the most successful sales trainers and sales performers in the world. His techniques, ideas, principles, and viewpoints have impacted the success of thousands. Yet, he readily and eagerly shares with you his failures and "less-than-successful" experiences so that he can underscore the wisdom gained. Tony failed on his way to success.

And you will, too. As countless people have proven: The faster you fail, the faster you will succeed.

2

WHO'S WHO IN YOUR TARGET ORGANIZATION?

If you can't begin to formulate a good answer to this all-important question, you're probably better off not trying to set the second meeting at all.

Let's face facts. It's all very well to say we want to win the second meeting. But *who,* exactly, should we be trying to include in the meeting after we've made initial face-to-face or telephone contact with the organization?

The way we *target* the second meeting will also determine how likely we are to hold on to the sale once it (seems to) come our way. We have to understand who's who in the target organization, or risk losing the sale.

During my training seminars, I always ask participants the question: *Who here has ever lost a sale after you had been told that you'd won it?*

At this point, a good many of the people in the audience put their hands up. If I'm not training people who are completely new to sales, and if the group is honest with themselves, then every hand will go up. My guess is that this "losing-the-sale-after-you've-won-it" problem has happened to you, just as it's happened to me.

Now here's my next question: *Why* does it happen?

To answer that, we need to understand the playing field that we've been invited to play on in the prospect's organization. It is a field that has many players with many different agendas. Sometimes it amazes me that we salespeople can get *any* sale to stick!

To make matters even more complicated, *each one* of the individuals in the different categories you'll be learning about in this chapter have varying levels of influence and authority when it comes to making the sale a reality. Before I introduce you to each of the categories of the people you *could* be meeting with, let's get a clearer understanding of the terminology we'll be using.

TARGET PEOPLE WITH INFLUENCE

For the purposes of our discussion, *influence* means having the ability to change the mind of one or more players in the organization. People with influence should be on our list of contacts for our first and subsequent meetings.

Influence is a powerful force that can make—or kill—a sale. Consider the following true story:

> By all indications, I was positioned as the vendor of choice for the procurement of a computerized automatic tester at a company I'll call Acme Corporation. This complex piece of equipment that I was selling made it possible to test electronic assemblies 200 times faster than organizations using traditional "technicians" to perform the same tests. More to the point, this technology eliminated jobs and got the product out the door faster.
>
> During my sales process at Acme, there was a young college intern working in the engineering department who attended all of the meetings and presentations that I conducted. He sat quietly taking notes, organizing and distributing action items. He was a nonplayer as far as I was concerned. He was not even on the payroll, hardly worth spending much time with. When he posed what seemed to be inconsequential questions, I gave short, dismissive answers.

Basically, I wrote him off. It wasn't my responsibility to babysit this kid. He could find out what he needed from the real players on the team. Such was my thinking, anyway. And it cost me the sale.

When I reached the "bottom of the ninth inning," with this account—when I was in what I thought was the final phase of the sale—guess what happened? One of my biggest competitors showed up. As it happened, this competitor was able to change the course of the sale and win the deal . . . after I had set the stage and done all of the heavy lifting!

Why did it happen? Because I hadn't targeted my second and subsequent meetings properly. Because I hadn't included that "kid" in the group of influencers I was winning over to my side. Several weeks later, just after I had recovered psychologically from the trauma of telling my manager that I had lost one of the biggest deals of my year to the competition, I learned that *my competitor's equipment had been in the engineering lab at the college of the "nonplayer"—that intern I had ignored.* He came in with a predisposition toward an existing brand, and I had done nothing to counter that predisposition. In fact, I didn't even know he had the predisposition.

It gets worse. This supposed "nonplayer" turned out to be the son of the president of the company.

Believe me when I tell you that *targeting the right people is everything* when it comes to second and subsequent meetings. Influence makes or breaks every sale. You must do your best to determine the *true* roles of all the individuals with whom you come in contact during the sales process. Each will have varying amounts of influence. It's your job to find out how much each person can really do when it comes to changing the minds of others, and then to target your eventual second meeting request accordingly.

TARGET PEOPLE WITH AUTHORITY

Authority means having the power to make decisions. People with authority—formal and informal—should be on our list of contacts for second and subsequent meetings.

The very idea of *authority* is easy to misunderstand. Consider, for the sake of argument, the president of a fully funded start-up operation. Surely this person has, for all intents and purposes, all the authority necessary to approve a computer system necessary to run the entire venture. Right? Not necessarily, as the following true story shows.

Some years back, I met with the president of such a company. This fast-growing start-up faced all the challenges that the system that I happened to be selling could meet. It was a match made in heaven. I had read about the company in the local business journal. The president's picture was on the front cover. I quickly had the front page matted and framed. I sent the framed picture to the president with a quick note presenting both the gift . . . and my idea for the company's next level of success. I made a quick call to the assistant, and one short week later I was walking into the president's office for my first appointment. What did I see? Prominently displayed on the wall above his credenza was (you guessed it) the framed and matted picture I had sent him.

Everything moves faster when you start at the top of an organization and move downward. This was the generally reliable principle I operated under, and thus it was that I rejoiced when this enlightened chief executive quickly accepted all of my ideas. Nods from (what I imagined were) "all the other key players" were plentiful, and the sales cycle accelerated. I saw myself moving into the final stages of the sale.

A scant two months later, which was lightning speed in my industry, I thought I had reached the promised land. As I sat in the same office of the same president (yes, the framed picture was still hanging there). I slid the purchase order across his desk and said, with great confidence, the following words: "Mr. Smith, every member of your team that we've met with is in full agreement: this is the right solution for you. All you need to do is sign our agreement, and the overachievement of your strategic initiatives for the year will become a reality. Your new computer system will be delivered, installed, and operational by your deadline of June 1st."

His response should have given me pause, but it didn't. He said: "Tell you what. I have a board meeting tonight. Come back tomorrow morning at 9:00 and you can pick the purchase order up from Tommie, my assistant."

Never one to question authority, I did as I was told. I left the office of the president, did a few cartwheels back to my company car, drove to the nearest ice cream store, bought a very large ice-cream cake, walked into my office, and threw a mid-afternoon party for my team. We had won! And in only two months! This was easily the shortest sales cycle in the history of our office! Everybody celebrated. . . . Too soon.

At nine the next morning, I waltzed back into the office of what I imagined was my new customer. But, instead of a purchase order, Mr. Smith's assistant had only grim news for me. The president was not available. There would be no purchase order for me to pick up. The board had not "approved" the purchase. One of the board members, it turned out, was a major stockholder in IBM (my biggest competitor). Her preference had been for an IBM system.

> Everything picks up speed when it goes downhill. The higher you make your first call, the faster your sales cycle will be.

How could something so sure, so real, vaporize? Simple. Somebody I hadn't talked to—a board member—had a higher level of authority than the president did. I later learned that that board member was the first investor, and had the biggest stake in the company.

I had celebrated just a bit too early. At the very least, I should have understood who was on the board and tried, early on in the relationship, for a meeting with some or all of these all-important individuals. But I never even asked for that meeting.

My manager never let me forget that lesson. I'd like for you to remember it, too.

TARGET PEOPLE WITH THE AUTHORITY TO APPROVE

For the purposes of our discussion, approval means having the ability to spend the amount of money it will take to purchase whatever you're selling without having to consult anyone else. People with approval should be on our list of contacts for first and subsequent meetings.

Those who possess extreme levels of approval can spend money not only without any else's authorization, but regardless of restrictions of budget that might hinder others in the organization! The buck really does stop on the desk of the approver.

Here's a true story about approval that will show you how important it is to target these people early on in your sales process.

One magnificent morning, the CEO of the largest telecommunications company in the world answered his own phone and took my call. What a surprise that was! Earlier in the week, I had sent a letter stating that I would call the CEO on that specific day, date, and time. Was he sitting at his desk eagerly waiting for my call? No. But that's not important. *He* picked up the phone, which was what mattered most to me.

I quickly stated my value proposition. He remembered the letter I'd sent, and he instructed me to contact three divisional presidents to see if they saw value in my proposition. Before he ended the call and returned to his busy day, I asked the one question that this CEO would love to have every salesperson in his organization asking the prospects they call on. I asked him: "If any of your three divisional presidents are personally convinced that my ideas will work for them, could you see yourself approving an expense of six hundred and fifty dollars for each one of your salespeople between now and the end of this calendar quarter, to be spent with my organization?"

Then, I did something I learned to do as a kid. I simply shut up and waited to see what would happen. (This, too, is a critical selling skill!)

There was a short pause, which seemed like a lifetime. I kept my mouth closed, then listened as the CEO said: "I can't see why not."

I wished him a prosperous day and concluded the call. I then began three sales cycles with each of his divisional presidents. Within three months, I landed a national contract to the tune of $650,000. This was and still is the largest single sale in the history of my company.

It's difficult to describe what it felt like to make that sale. "Pure nirvana" comes pretty darn close. What I want you to notice here, though, is that in my initial *and subsequent* meetings, I was able to appeal to my initial conversation with the ultimate source of approval in the organization. He was as good as his word—and he made not only my initial face-to-face meetings with key people possible, but also every subsequent meeting.

SECOND MEETINGS AND THE "TRILOGY" OF YOUR SALES CYCLE

Your sales cycle unfolds over a number of face-to-face meetings. If the relationship stops after the first meeting, there is no sales cycle.

Influence, authority, and approval are three of the most important components of your sales cycle. When you target people who fit all three profiles, you can accelerate your sales process, get more second meetings, and make the job of selling more pleasurable and more profitable.

If you *don't* target people who fit these three profiles, your funnel looks lousy, sales drop off, your forecast is off, and your sales manager starts looking at you with a puzzled or somewhat funny look on their face.

The choice is yours.

Put the power of this trilogy to work for you. Figure out who's who in the target organization, and try to hook up with the right people as soon as possible in your sales cycle. If you find out the right information about your target company and build people with influence, authority, and approval into your second and subsequent meetings, *you will close more sales.*

REALITY CHECK: YOUR HOTTEST PROSPECT

Think of the hottest prospect that is currently in your sales funnel. Ask yourself the following questions:

1. What is the name and title of the individual with the greatest influence that I know?

    Name: _____ Title: _____

2. What is the name and title of the individual with the greatest authority to approve that I know?

    Name: _____ Title: _____

> The person with the most influence and authority will buy from you in two sales calls.

Be ruthlessly honest—how well have you targeted the key players in this account? What meaningful information were you able to develop as the result of the first phone call or face-to-face meetings? What *should* you have uncovered in the first call or meeting?

Roll-up your sleeves and turn to the next chapter!

FROM COACH STEVE

Do you have the courage and confidence to engage with anyone, at any level, of your target organizations?

Take a minute to think about this question. Your reflex answer is probably, "Sure!" My challenge to you is to look at your historical sales efforts. Have you ever handed off the sales process to someone in the prospect organization hoping that they would "carry the deal to the decision maker"? Have you started "low" in your prospect companies hoping to "work your way up" to a "yes"? Have you been satisfied with smaller deals because you are going for "low hanging fruit" just to "get a foot in the door"?

If you recognize any of these tendencies, welcome to human nature. You see, by design we are all wired for "expedience." Built deep into our nervous system is the tendency to look for the "shortest or easiest route between two points."

It is not that we are lazy or that we lack ambition. In fact, it may be quite the opposite! We are ambitiously looking for the shortest, easiest route between where we are . . . and where we want to go.

But there's the principle we often overlook, a principle that I want to help you implant firmly into your new way of thinking about selling as you work through Tony's program: **Quick and easy is usually not synonymous with success.**

Building confidence requires that you challenge yourself to do more or work harder than you have in the past. Tony's suggestions may look like hard work or more effort than you are used to. Take him up on the challenge! The result will be a new "muscle" or, at very least, new strength in your selling muscles. Stretch yourself to go a slightly different route between where you are and making the sale. Challenge yourself to working through the process more strategically, more thoughtfully. Allow Tony's suggestions to compel you to experiment.

What you will discover will be a trail not many sales professionals travel—only those that reach peak performance.

3

FOUR CATEGORIES

There are, by my count, four categories of people you will eventually have to deal with throughout your sales process. Getting a second appointment is part of the sales process, so it's in your best interest to know who these people are and to be ready to interact with them at any time. The four categories are:

1. Recommender.
2. Influencer.
3. Decision Maker.
4. Approver.

We'll get into what each group *does* in just a moment. What's important right now is that the presence of people in any one or more of these categories may not always be immediately apparent to you. People in one of these four categories may be influencing the outcome of your sale—without your even knowing it!

SILENT ADVERSARIES, SILENT ALLIES

We defined *influence* as the ability to change the minds of others. Make no mistake, people in these four categories can and do exercise influence on buying decisions that may undermine your efforts to win the second appointment—and, eventually, the sale.

You must take into account the work of *silent adversaries* in four different categories—people with their own agendas who can be poison to any sale. On the other hand, a couple of *silent allies* can help you carry the day. Both silent adversaries and silent allies will be found in the ranks of the company you're trying to turn into a customer. It's within these four categories that your attempt to secure the second appointment—and ultimately the sale—will be won or lost.

Let's look now at the four roles and their four agendas—as well as the best ways to interact with these people (once you've identified them) so getting the second appointment is easier and so that the time and effort you put into that meeting will be more likely to yield the result you want: a sale.

THE ROLE OF THE RECOMMENDER

Have you ever seen a suggestion box soliciting your opinion or ideas for improving service or the quality of a product?

Have you ever received a survey form that gave you a perk (for instance, 1,000 bonus miles on some airline) if you passed along your "candid" opinion?

> It's the silent objection that your prospect listens the most to.

Have you ever been asked to serve as a member of a committee that was given the task to "brainstorm" some new ideas on how to do something?

If you answered yes to any of those questions, congratulations. You've had the privilege of being asked to play the role of a Recommender.

In each organization we try to sell to, there are large groups of people who spend their days actually *doing* what other people plan, outline, set up, and evaluate. These folks—whether receptionists, assistants, editors, analysts, or contributors in any other category— may well be invited to play the role of the Recommender and thus can have an impact on your efforts to win commitments.

Recommenders can be found just about anywhere in an organization, from the janitor's room to the boardroom. Education level, gender, talent, or intelligence quotient matter not—anyone and everyone can be a Recommender. What *does* matter is this: Recommenders make recommendations (often based on direct experience) that can carry a great deal of weight. But they don't *always* carry a great deal of weight. Any recommendation is like an opinion: It can be followed—or ignored.

How many times have you been involved in a sale whereby you worked your fanny off jumping through all the hoops, providing information and proof of concept to a committee (a group of Recommenders) and learned in the end that the group recommended *nothing at all?*

What's happening in those situations? The "need" went away; the project was "deprioritized"; the group simply lost interest. These are all realistic possibilities.

In the world of sales, the impact of the Recommender can be volatile. Sands shift, needs come and go. But the Recommenders themselves may well stick around. Often, you'll notice some familiar faces as fresh evaluations are sought out, interest in "new" projects is rekindled, and "fresh" initiatives look a great deal like the initiatives of yesteryear, yestermonth, or even yesterday.

This game can get pretty frustrating. As a salesperson, you have to rehash what appears, for all the world, to be the same thing you presented to the Recommender(s) last time around. In fact, it's more the rule than the exception that organizations and teams of Recommenders embark on "exploratory evaluations" that appear (to the outsider) to be very real sales opportunities indeed—but are simply fact-finding missions conducted with the knowledge that salespeople won't do much research work for you unless they think there's a chance they can make the sale.

The Recommender's Agenda

Despite their occasional dilatory ways when it comes to dealing with salespeople, Recommenders long for recognition and acknowledgment. If there was ever a group who wanted their voices to be heard, Recommenders are that group.

For the most part, Recommenders feel like mushrooms—they're kept in the dark and nourished on a great deal of fertilizer. They often know what's going on "on the ground," but are less certain about the grand initiatives of the people they're sharing their recommendations with. Because they are typically the *users* of the systems in the enterprise, they know what's working and what's not. They are, as a general rule, honest and trusting . . . they are usually happy to share with you all the information you need to implement your solution, assuming it's ever actually purchased.

THE INFLUENCER'S ROLE

Influencers live to be right.

Influencers are, not infrequently, technical experts who love to win arguments and prove that all the facts are exactly as they've described them; they get a special pleasure from arguing a certain position. They get a charge out of the praise and recognition that comes from correctly identifying the problem and the solution. If they were k-nines in a competition, Influencers would be the ones who were totally committed to being named "best in breed."

As a rule, Influencers tend be fairly critical about any new initiative. They may be scientists or engineers—these are the folks who look to *disprove* all competing ideas, remove them by the process of elimination, and in so doing, prove their own point. (They often deny that this is how they operate and offer arguments to *disprove* the contentions of people who say otherwise.)

Influencers also make a habit of guarding their information and criteria. Unlike Recommenders, they make you connect all the dots yourself. They play things very close to the vest; they know the rules, and they know how to follow them to their best advantage.

Avoid asking Influencers questions such as:

- "Who else are you looking at?"
- "May I have a copy of your evaluation matrix?"
- "Are you open to input from/discussions with one of our technical people?"

> Never ask Influencers questions that put them on the spot.

These appeals almost always fall on deaf ears when you're dealing with Influencers and may well make securing the second meeting, or anything else, more difficult. (Questions like these can earn you a reputation as an agitator with Influencers.)

As if things weren't difficult enough already, you must remember to avoid making any statement or posing any question that even vaguely resembles criticism of these folks or their ideas. Although they can be extremely critical, Influencers do *not* appreciate being criticized.

How can you win with these people? Simply by focusing on helping them *eliminate* problems. Influencers live to spot errors and inconsistencies. Identify potential flaws in *other people's ideas* (not your ideas, not the ideas of the Influencer you're working with), and you'll stand a decent chance of turning this potential adversary into an ally.

The Influencer's Agenda

The agenda here, as you've probably already gathered, is pretty simple: Shoot holes in other people's arguments—and win recognition for being correct. That's about it.

Warning: If you don't have an Influencer who is on your side in every suspect and prospect organization you connect with, *it will be extremely difficult to make the sale.* Instead, you will spend countless hours jumping through hoops, proving your ideas with presentations, and assuming, incorrectly, that "that looks interesting" means "that looks like something we might buy."

Find an Influencer early on in your sales process, prove your credential as an error-spotting ally, and help this person influence whoever needs to be influenced about the merits of your solution.

It will take a concerted effort on your part to recruit an Influencer. Typically, these folks *will not* help you sell, so don't succumb to the temptation to "leave everything in their hands." They may, however, work closely with you and make (critically important) technical endorsements on your behalf once they decide you can help them make their case in a given area.

Point to ponder: In my many years of selling, I have yet to meet an Influencer who was once, or ever wanted to be, a salesperson.

THE DECISION MAKER'S ROLE

In today's business world, the Decision Maker is the person who can endorse something a Recommender or that the Influencer signs off on . . . and make a yes decision about implementing the solution.

Once the Decision Maker makes a yes decision, the Decision Maker passes the matter along to the Approver for the *approval,* which we'll discuss later. When we get a no answer from the Decision Maker, that only means someone else (such as our competition) has gotten the yes. It's important to understand that the job of the Decision Maker is to say yes. Contrary to popular belief, these people do not have veto power for the opportunity and/or corporate strategic initiative. That ultimate veto power belongs to the Approver.

I was 44 years old when I first learned the real importance of finding and qualifying the Decision Maker. My teacher was a C-level executive of a manufacturing company, a prospect of mine. His company made survival vessels used on oil rigs and platforms in the North Sea and other harsh, remote areas. The egg-shaped vessels could hold an entire crew of workers. If a disaster took place on the platform (e.g., an uncontrollable firestorm), the crew would enter the vessel, batten down the hatches, and hit the "launch" button, which would catapult them into the ocean, 60 feet below. The vessel was fireproof, crash proof, and highly seaworthy. It was the first vehicle of its kind, and it was revolutionary in the open-sea rescue arena.

The company's first customer, an early adopter, was the largest oil exploration company in the world. What was I selling my C-level guy? The entire launch platform and instrumentation required for successfully deploying and navigating the "egg." My total solution for each oil platform was about $350,000. The end user wanted an initial quantity of 100 "survival systems." At the time, I was pulling down a commission-only salary of 7.5 percent. This looked like heaven on earth—my own oil well. I quickly began to look at new homes and property. I figured I needed a place to put all those commission dollars that would be coming my way.

I had, over the past 16 months, put my deal entirely in the hands of this C-level executive. I had qualified him, his organization, and the deal. I was, in fact, the sole source provider of the equipment that his organization *needed* to satisfy the oil company's requirements. I saw no need to learn anything about the oil business or to meet the end user that *my* customer was selling to.

During the final stages of the sale, when I was within weeks of those commission checks, I got a call. The deal had suddenly fallen through. Mr. C-level walked away from the biggest deal his organization would ever see and in the process took my enormous commission check with him. He had taken a hard line during the price negotiations and refused to lower his price by 20 percent.

He thought the oil company didn't have a choice because of industry compliance regulations that they were faced with by year end. He thought that his prospect *had* to make the deal work at the higher price. Mr. C's hard line on the price backfired and cost me the deal from heaven.

The real authority in this case was not my guy, but the end user, whom I had studiously ignored. In the end, the oil company got what it was after and met its compliance deadline—but didn't use my company's equipment to do so. If I had covered the bases properly and qualified all the parties involved, I would have taken steps to make sure that the end user specified my launch and navigation system. But I didn't do that. I failed to *identify* and *qualify* the actual Decision Maker. As a result, I lost the deal.

The Decision Maker's Agenda

If you remember one fact about Decision Makers, remember this: Their big win happens when *you* win the sale and deliver the results you promise. Why? Because they want the publicity! They want to be the hero!

For the most part, Decision Makers are upwardly mobile, highly visible types—and they want to stay that way. They are almost always politically astute, and they love to broadcast positive news stories about themselves to all levels of the organization. At higher levels, you'll find that Decision Makers are essentially fearless! They know the terrain, they know the political climate, and they know how to navigate it to their own best advantage.

Or so it seems to them. The careers of these people can actually be fairly volatile, and many Decision Makers move around quite a bit. Your most helpful Decision Makers come from your existing customer base. As these loyal and thankful individuals move from company to company in pursuit of new career opportunities, they take their loyalty to you with them. Call them at their new office and ask: "Are you ready to achieve similar or even better results here at New Company than we accomplished over at Old Company?"

Bingo! Your sales cycle launches, and your Decision Maker is in place once again.

THE APPROVER'S ROLE

The Approver sits at the top of the corporate totem pole. Approvers are individuals whom I respectfully refer to as VITOs: *Very Important Top Officers*. I wrote about them at length in my first book on sales.

These VITOs—who may have titles such as chief executive officer, owner, senator, chief of police, or some other variation on Top Banana—have the ultimate *veto* power. That makes them the ultimate Approvers.

Whatever you choose to call this person, keep in mind that the Approver, with some exceptions such as government agencies, the military, or municipalities, has no limits, no budget, and no one to get that approval from. Power, control, and authority are critically important to these folks, and because of that they tend to be very fast on their feet and very decisive.

Very often, the VITO (or Approver, to use our current parlance) supports any strategic corporate initiatives that, when accomplished, will assist them in the *overachievement* of their vision.

Approvers pick the appropriate person on their team of Decision Makers (whatever their actual title) and empower the person to look at all the tactical ways to make the vision a reality—by a certain deadline. Their command might sound something like this: *"I need greater control and visibility! Find me the best accounting system in the world that will do the job and fit the budget."*

So it is that the Decision Maker of choice (maybe the chief financial officer) appoints an Influencer to assemble a Recommender (e.g., a head accountant) or a group of Recommenders (representatives from the credit department, accounting, order entry, customer services, collections, etc.). These folks are then commanded to "find every single accounting package in the world that exceeds our needs and is under budget." If you have an eagle eye, you just

> The Approver has the ultimate veto power over all decisions.

picked up on the addition of two key phrases to the initiative: "exceeds our needs" (rather than "best accounting system in the world") and "under budget" (rather than "fit the budget"). The additions are concepts that Decision Makers are likely to throw into the equation—not Approvers.

You see the pattern. The Approver issues strategic commands that the Decision Maker of choice then takes tactical steps on to make happen.

> Decision
> Makers are
> empowered to
> say yes; make
> sure they say it
> to you.

Decision Makers think and act in terms that relate to tactics. Approvers think and act in terms that relate to strategies.

Decision Makers, in most every case, try to convince you that they are also the *Approver* of the sale. That's not true.

From our point of view, it's easy to want to believe that our sales job ends when the decision is made in our favor. And it's easy to see why the Decision Maker wants us to think that way. If you take the time to look at all of the contracts and/or agreements that you've won, you'll most likely see the name(s) of the Decision Maker on the signature line of the contract. You may then be tempted to say to yourself (or someone else): "See, Joe Smith is the Approver. He signed for the $400,000 network."

WRONG!

The Approver actually made Joe sign that contract. Why? Because that's the best way for any Approver to empower key team members—and put the responsibility for final execution on someone else's back. The real power, nevertheless, lies with the Approver.

Decision Makers are not intentionally lying to us when they tell us that the "buck stops here." Actually, they love answering the question that we salespeople have been taught to ask: "Who besides you will be making this decision?" When we ask that question, they get to answer, "No one."

And they believe it. But the reason that they believe it is that the Approver has talked them into believing it.

These days, Approvers have a huge role in purchase decisions, far greater than most salespeople imagine. Ten years ago, it was common for a vice president of finance to have independent authority and approval for purchases up to, perhaps, $250,000. Today, that same VP has formal authority to spend something on the order of $250. Our contacts are not about to come clean and tell us this, but it's the truth.

The Approver's Agenda

Any Approver sitting at the top of any ethically run, successful organization has a mission: to be focused on every activity that could conceivably affect profitability and/or shareholder value.

For Approvers, it all boils down to fundamental questions: What revenue is coming in and what expenses are going out? What is the market share? How recognizable is the company brand (or goodwill)?

My personal experience is that Approvers in similar market niches have similar goals and tend to use similar language. Therefore, if you want to tap into what they like to talk about and what their hot buttons are, I invite you to become an industry/niche/marketplace expert. Go out and talk to five Approvers in any one industry and ask them what their specific goals, plans, and objectives are during the next month, quarter, or fiscal year. Then ask them to explain to you what they personally see as their major challenges in *overaccomplishing* those goals. (Don't worry—Approvers love to talk about this stuff.)

I'll guarantee you that the sixth Approver you speak to will magically fall in line with the other five!

LOCK IN WHAT YOU'VE LEARNED

I invite you to participate in an e-learning exercise that I've developed based on this chapter. Visit www.gettingthesecondappointment .com and click on Chapter 3's Online Assets. You'll get the chance to accurately identify the Recommender, Influencer, Decision Maker, and Approver for every sales opportunity you have.

Let's push on to the next chapter, shall we?

4

SELLING ACROSS THE ENTERPRISE

To win a second meeting, you must be able to broadcast value to various folks who hold various positions in the target organizations.

I call this process of broadcasting value to more than one person "selling across the enterprise." In this chapter, we look at three principles for doing this successfully.

PRINCIPLE 1: THINK OUTSIDE THE OWNER'S MANUAL

In some cases, selling across the enterprise means knowing how to talk about using what you sell in a way that varies from the "owner's manual." What company successes can you broadcast along these lines to help make a meeting with someone *other than* your primary contact more likely?

This is not as difficult a strategy for setting up a second meeting as it might sound . . . assuming that you're willing to open yourself up to the input, experiences, and referrals of your potential customers on the first meeting. I've sold a good many things over the years, and one iron-sure principle I've come to rely on is that, given enough time, my customers could figure out ways to use my stuff that neither I nor the marketing department of the company

I worked for would ever have thought of in a million years. But to implement those solutions, I had to be willing to follow the lead of my customers, which meant I had to be ready to use my ears.

When I was selling high-tech computer systems, for instance, my customers never ceased to amaze my design engineers with various new applications they discovered. These were applications that were never designed into the equipment. Every time I thought I had totally gotten all of the business imaginable from these existing accounts, I'd find about some new way of using what I sold from one of my customers. Often, I'd learn about the existence of a whole new department full of potential users, complete with budgets, who had the potential to buy my stuff and put it to new and exciting uses.

I wish I could tell you that I always converted these opportunities and built new inroads into my existing customer base. The fact is, though, I frequently got complacent with my "real" business, and, in so doing, left the door open for the competition. Don't make the same mistake I did. Reach out to every constituency you can think of within the target organization.

At the same time you're doing this, however, you should be sure to obey. . . .

PRINCIPLE 2: INVEST YOUR TIME INTELLIGENTLY

Why on earth was my office phone ringing at 6:00 in the morning?

That was the question I asked myself one very early morning. I picked up the phone, expecting to hear the voice of my brother from New Jersey, getting his day started at the crack of 9:00 and looking for a chance to engage in some small talk.

> You can't just think outside the box...you have to act outside it.

It wasn't my brother, though. It was the chief engineer of a fully funded start-up company calling to ask me for a meeting. The company was creating enormous water desalinization units that converted salt water to fresh water; the machines were powered by the movement of waves in the ocean. These self-propelled giants were to be used to provide drinking water in remote islands to support military troops or other temporary inhabitants in times of emergencies. My new prospect told me that he was a past user and familiar with my company's top-of-the-line scientific equipment.

"Could you come out this morning, meet the team, and work up a quote for me?" he asked.

Instantly, I responded "Sure!"

Actually, I had two appointments at existing accounts that morning, as well as a sales meeting. All three commitments, I figured, could be either rescheduled or blown off, given this more important opportunity that I saw falling into my lap at the break of dawn. It would take me an hour to get there, which gave me ample time to gather up some data sheets and my presentation materials, price list, and configuration guide, but that was all going to be time very well spent. After all, I was going to meet the team and work up a quote. This company was presold, and it was presold on me. If meeting everyone of consequence in this account wasn't worth my time and effort, what was?

I was out the door in a flash. There were no fewer than six people in attendance. Over the course of a three-hour meeting, I covered every single aspect of my company and our system for those six people. I bonded. I communicated. I built bridges. The meeting was going so well that, at one point, I conferenced in a new product manager from our company to talk about our not-quite-done, not-yet-released future products for this exciting new customer-in-training. Sure, my manager disapproved of such "selling of futures," but *this* situation was different. *This* sale was moving fast, and I needed to break a few rules.

I left the meeting flying high. My new prospect had been eager to listen, had been anxious to understand every aspect of my configuration, and (best of all) had accepted my pricing without batting an eye. I had ballparked my future product's price—on the high side—and gotten nothing but smiles and positive body language. We had agreed to get back together in one week's time.

This sale was a dream come true. I immediately placed this new contact on my sales forecast at a 75 percent probability. I talked the sale up with my manager and got a well-deserved reprieve for missing the other commitments I'd had that morning.

What I'd failed to notice was that, although I was selling across the enterprise, although I had a commitment for a second meeting, and although I had developed all the enthusiasm for the sale anyone could possibly have desired, I didn't really know that much about the company I was supposedly selling to. I'd spent the entire meeting talking about *my* stuff, answering questions about *my* equipment. I'd been doing all the talking. This should have been a tip-off that I was not investing my time wisely with this particular prospect, but I missed the signal.

I'll make a long story short and save myself the pain of telling you every detail of the five additional presentations I delivered for this company. I won't break down the engineering time I committed to evaluating the project. I won't tell you how much I spent to fly my new product manager in to discuss future products. I'll just tell you that the company never bought a damned thing from me.

Why, then, you might ask, did my "prospect" invest all that time in attending my five presentations and meeting the new product manager? The truth is, they weren't investing anything. I was.

My contacts at that company never had the slightest intention of buying anything from me. Instead, they were in search of a free education that would enable them to tweak the offering of their vendor of choice (whom they had already identified). They reached out to me—and pumped me for information—to use my volumes of (borderline-confidential) data to obtain free consulting services that would help them finalize what they were getting from someone else. I freely, willingly, and insanely gave my "prospect" this information.

The moral: Be suspicious if the deal looks too good to be true, if the prospect's encouraging you to do *all* (or nearly all) of the talking, and if you don't (or can't) develop solid information about who else the company is looking at as a prospective vendor. I was too excited to take the time to bother with these concerns, and, as a result, I got burned.

Before you invest your valuable time with a new contact who "definitely" plans to buy from you, do a reality check. Take the time to find out whether you're selling or just giving someone a free education.

PRINCIPLE 3: THINK LIFETIME VALUE—BY ALIGNING YOUR SALES PROCESS TO THE ORGANIZATION

Every account in your territory, whether it reflects a prospect or an existing customer, has what I like to call a "lifetime value" that either you or a competitor will tap into. Every enterprise has within it a value that is directly proportional to your ability to sell across the enterprise. This value will depend on your willingness to put in the work necessary to connect with people in different areas of the organization, to understand and qualify their real needs, and to develop that enterprise into a loyal, ever-expanding, and growing long-term business relationship.

> Lifetime value is the total amount of revenue and referral your customer is willing to give to you.

Someone is going to understand, and make the most of, the enterprise's lifetime value. The question is: Is it going to be you, or is it going to be your competition?

To make sure the answer to that question is the one you want it to be, you have to incorporate four new and different steps into your sales process— the four essential steps of enterprise selling:

1. *Exploring:* Performing precall, prequalifying research.
2. *Initiating:* Gathering critical enterprise-specific requirements.
3. *Sponsoring:* Getting on the right person's agenda (in terms of both time and topic).
4. *Leveraging:* Becoming the "brainchild" of choice.

As you ponder these four and perhaps unfamiliar steps, let me ask you a question: What's the title that appears under your name on your business card? Is it account manager? account executive? account representative? Is it any other trumped-up title that intentionally avoids the word *selling, sales,* or *salesperson?*

If so, you're not alone. More than 90 percent of salespeople do not have the word *salesperson* on their card for at least three reasons:

1. With very few exceptions, the people salespeople most often give their cards to *hate* salespeople.
2. Most of the activities such salespeople perform are not considered selling activities. I'm talking about activities such as: solving customer problems, training the customer on the use of products, customer care, and performing administrative tasks (such as forecasts, expense reports, CRM busy work, attending meetings, account reviews).
3. Some combination of 1 and 2.

Look again at the four new elements of enterprisewide selling you just learned about. Notice that only the last two connect directly with activities traditionally identified with "selling":

- *Exploring:* Nonselling.
- *Initiating:* Nonselling.
- *Sponsoring:* Selling.
- *Leveraging:* Selling.

Now, look at the four levels of the business hierarchy you found out about in Chapter 3. Notice that they exist in every enterprise in the world and that they align perfectly with the enterprise selling process that taps into the lifetime value of the account:

> We must direct our selling activities to individuals who love to be sold to.

- *Exploring* includes nonselling with the Recommender to learn about the target organization.
- *Initiating* includes nonselling with the Influencer to determine critical enterprise-specific requirements.
- *Sponsoring* includes selling with the Decision Maker to get on the right person's agenda.
- *Leveraging* includes selling with the Approver to become the provider of choice.

We're not "selling" or making a "sales call" (at least, not in the way these words are traditionally understood) when we're exploring or initiating, and we *are* "selling" whenever we're sponsoring and leveraging.

We put ourselves and our organizations in a better position to tap into the lifetime value of the account if we match up the right activity with the right contact on the first, second, and subsequent meetings.

You read right. If we really want to get more—and more meaningful—second appointments, and if we really want to land bigger sales (enterprisewide) that maximize the account's lifetime value, we have to be sure we're aligning what we do with the proper person in the organization.

> Top performers spend 70 percent of their time on *selling activities* and 30 percent on *nonselling activities.* What's your mix?

LOCK IN WHAT YOU'VE LEARNED

I invite you to participate in an e-learning exercise that I've developed based on this chapter. Visit www.gettingthesecondappointment .com and click on Chapter 4 Online Assets. You'll get a chance to download a cool form to calculate your customer's lifetime value and other valuable information.

Turn to the next chapter.

5

PATHWAYS TO THE RIGHT SECOND APPOINTMENT

In the previous chapter, we saw how traditional definitions of *selling* (e.g., presenting a recommendation or canvassing for new business) really don't encompass all the activities we have to undertake in today's marketplace to attract and retain customers. If you were to pick up a dictionary or thesaurus right now, you'd actually find some very narrow ideas—and even a few stereotypically negative concepts—in answer to the question, "What is selling?"

Here's my definition of the profession of selling:

Representing your products, services, and solutions in the best interest of the other person or party—so that their requirements, needs, and visions are overachieved in a time frame that they define.

I am more comfortable with this definition than with any other I've come across, because it actually reflects what I should have been doing in the first 10 years of my selling career . . . and what I actually learned to do successfully in the 18 years following.

(I can't take full credit for the definition you just read. In preparation for writing this book, I polled my very best customers about their definition of selling, and I also talked with guests that I've had on my radio and Internet talk shows and asked them for their opinions about the matter. What you just read is a combined effort of more than 200 suggestions.)

There are four activities that can help us to implement this newer, more accurate definition of selling when we're pursuing second appointments (or any other sign of progress in the sales relationship). *Only two of the four involve making "buy" recommendations.*

Let's look in depth at all four activities.

EXPLORING

To explore means to search out, to investigate the unknown, to learn something new. Every time you connect with someone with the intent of getting information, you are engaged in the task of exploring.

Associate the following words with selling: Helpful, caring, consultative, constructive, guidance, needs, vision, and overachievement.

Exploring typically means asking questions such as: "Tell me all about how your business operates." "How many employees work here?" "How many different locations do you have?" "How much do you think you spend each month on network services?" "How many output devices do you currently have in your department?"

Quick quiz: If you were to choose from our hierarchy of players (Recommender, Influencer, Decision Maker, or Approver), who would be your first choice for a conversational partner when it comes to exploring?

Please think of your best answer before you proceed.

• • •

If you said "Recommender," congratulations—you're on the right track. (If you came up with any other answer, please review Chapters 3 and 4.)

The Recommender is the person (or group of people) who can give you the information you need to set up the application of your product, service, or solution. Recommenders typically *will not* deliver decisions themselves on whether to use your product or service, and they may even resent being pressured to do so. The most important thing to bear in mind is that it's usually a waste of everyone's time trying to get these people to decide to buy from you.

Let's assume you're on the phone, trying to set your first appointment with a company you wish to sell to. You manage to strike up a pleasant conversation with a front-line person who would actually use what your company sells. This is a classic Recommender.

How might the discussion sound? Here are two possibilities (Initial chitchat about the Recommender's daily routine leads to your question):

SALESPERSON: How many times would you say you walk to your printer on the third floor to pick up your copies each day?

RECOMMENDER: Oh, probably between four and five.

SALESPERSON: And how long would you say that takes—maybe half an hour?

RECOMMENDER: That seems about right.

SALESPERSON: Okay. You know, you could save all of that time by installing our personal DeskScreen 1250 under your plasma display. After installation, each of your documents would cost only 3.944 cents each instead of the 6.5 cents you're probably currently spending. We have five different configurations, three of which can output full photo-quality color. If you give me your e-mail address, I can send you a PDF file that will demonstrate exactly how we . . . (blah, blah, blah . . .).

Or (Initial chitchat about the Recommender's daily routine leads to your question):

SALESPERSON: How many times would you say you walk to your printer on the third floor to pick up your copies each day?

RECOMMENDER: Oh, probably between four and five.

SALESPERSON: And how long would you say that takes—maybe half an hour?

RECOMMENDER: That seems about right.

SALESPERSON: Okay. What else should I know about the printer on the third floor?

RECOMMENDER: Well, it seems like it breaks down at least once each week. That's a pain, because people can't get the materials they need for team scheduling meetings.

SALESPERSON: Besides yourself, who else does this impact?

RECOMMENDER: Well, we've had two situations in the past quarter where production was delayed and three of our key customers didn't get their shipments on time.

SALESPERSON: Okay. Good to know. One last question. Who is the person in your organization who is held most responsible for the on-time delivery of your products?

RECOMMENDER: That would be Jessie Withers, our COO.

SALESPERSON: Got it. Thanks for your insights—have a great rest of the day.

Can you see the advantage the second exchange has over the first?

In the second dramatization, the salesperson got a ton of additional information—and didn't try to get the Recommender to buy anything. That's smart, because this person certainly lacks the authority to do so.

> Regardless of how much you "tell," you can't "sell" to someone who can't buy.

I think you'll realize that it makes good sense to pick your battles in the way I'm suggesting here. When we select the topic that actually matches the role of the player in our hierarchy, we're in a statistically better position to get the first appointment with the right person . . . and we're also in a better position to schedule (and maximize our selling opportunities during) the second appointment.

INITIATING

To initiate means "to begin to put into motion or to introduce knowledge relevant to the subject or discussion at hand."

Initiating is the point in our sales process where we begin to map our products, services, and solutions to the needs we've uncovered during our exploring activities.

Given the four players we're working with—Recommender, Influencer, Decision Maker, and Approver—who would be your first choice as the person or group to interact with when it comes to initiating?

Think of your best answer before you proceed.

• • •

We want to match our initiating sales activity with the Influencer(s), those analysts who serve, perhaps in addition to other formal roles, as the important advisors to the organization's Decision Makers and Approvers. (If you aligned this activity to anyone in the organization other than the Influencer, you may want to review the concepts covered in Chapters 3 and 4.)

It's important to understand what Influencers can—and can't—do for you. Anyone who's sold professionally for more than, for example, a year or so knows that these people, like Recommenders, are not the best people to target for buy decisions.

Think of your own experience. Have you ever had a meeting with someone who could influence the purchase decision and then noticed the conversation stopping dead in its tracks when you started to deliver your pitch?

Let's say you happen to be selling sophisticated spectrum analyzers that are used in cath labs in hospitals. You're sitting with the head radiologist discussing the attributes of your products. Here's what the conversation sounds like:

> Knowing what your prospect can and can't do for you will unlock the door to your sale.

SALESPERSON: (at the end of the meeting): Are there any other questions that come to mind about the compliance capabilities of our system?

INFLUENCER: No, I think that covers everything.

SALESPERSON: Great! Before we go any further, let me ask you something. Because compliance is important to you and because we're the only supplier that offers that capability, were you planning to look at any other manufacturers of spectrum analyzers before making your decision?

INFLUENCER: I am not at liberty to discuss that with you.

(An awkward, ominous pause follows before the Influencer excuses himself or herself and leaves the room.)

The meeting's original intent was to introduce knowledge—and that's what Influencers live for—exposure to new facts. Not surprisingly, the discussion was going along just fine. It ended, however, on the lowest possible note when the salesperson tried to use the relationship with the Influencer to confirm his or her position as the sole vendor being considered. In essence, the salesperson tried to get the Influencer to sign off on his or her "buy now" recommendation. Bad move.

Remember, the Influencer cannot make the decision to buy anything. The Influencer can, however, change the minds of those who can decide to buy whatever you have to offer. Respect that role—and never pressure an Influencer for a decision.

SPONSORING

What comes to mind when you think of the word *sponsor*?

For most people, sponsor calls to mind related words such as coach, champion, mentor, or backer. A sponsor is someone who may speak for or act on the behalf of someone else—someone who has a strong belief in another person or idea or will vouch for another's credibility.

> Sponsors help you sell ... don't ask them to make the sale for you.

When applied to our sales process, sponsoring means acting in such a way that the best interest of others can be served. This connects back to that definition of selling we looked at a little earlier.

Whenever we serve someone else's best interest, *our* best interest will in turn be served. When we sponsor our own sales process, we seek a sponsor within our prospect's and customer's organization. Given the four people in the organization we could be connecting with—Recommender, Influencer, Decision Maker, and Approver—who is the best candidate for us to target as the sponsor of our sales process?

Think of your best answer before you proceed.

• • •

You've got it. It's the Decision Maker whom we want to take on the role of sponsorship for the acquisition of our product, service, or solution.

Ideally, the Decision Maker is the person we want to have direct interaction with during the second meeting (or perhaps even earlier, during the first meeting or during premeeting interactions). This is the person we want to become our chief cheerleader and advocate. This is the person we want working on our behalf in seeking a favorable approval.

The reason that Decision Makers make perfect sponsors is that they know what's going on and who's making it happen. They have direct access up and down the hierarchy. It's not a problem for them to connect with the Approver and relate to the Influencers and Recommenders. Successful Decision Makers are in alignment with the entire enterprise and, for the most part, are upwardly mobile. They're the folks we want on our team.

Decision Makers who act as sponsors can be new contacts you make in the target organization; they can also be customers who respect what you've done for them either directly or indirectly in the past. Whether they're new or old allies, they must be strong believers in you and what you and your company represent. They must have a desire to see you succeed because they know that they will win when you do. (And once you pull off the seemingly impossible, they won't mind broadcasting your shared success to everyone else in the organization, either.)

When we interact with the Decision Maker, we are constantly matching and mapping our ideas to their personal and professional goals. We're learning what matters to them, exactly how they define victory. Then we're drawing as many parallels as possible between their vision of a "win" and the resources we've got that can make that vision a reality.

Recognition, image, reputation, stature, loyalty, honesty, and respect are important baselines in discussions with the Decision Makers. Once they start talking to you about this stuff, you have an ally—probably the most important ally in the organization.

Once you have such an ally, there's really only one important rule to follow: Tell your sponsor everything—the good, bad, and ugly. If you have delivery problems, tell your sponsor first. If you have product reliability issues, tell your sponsor first. If your organization is getting ready to stop supporting any particular revision of a product (such as a piece of software), pick up the phone and tell your sponsor the moment you learn of the decision.

Never let any news about you or your stuff get to your Decision Maker from any source other than you.

LEVERAGING

When you are leveraging, you are consciously drawing another person's attention to any one (or all) of the following circumstances:

1. Your products, services, and solutions can measurably add value to your prospect's/customer's enterprise.
2. You can clearly articulate and demonstrate (with referrals, case studies, and/or testimonials) that you can deliver this value.
3. Your conviction about your products, services, and solutions is unshakable and evident.

What do I mean by "value"? When any result you deliver is measured and articulated with a number or a percentage that's considered "hard-dollar value" (e.g., reducing the time it takes to go from concept to product launch by 35 percent or increased add-on business from existing accounts by $12,000 per account). There's also *soft-dollar value,* which reflects important organizational contributions that are more difficult to measure (e.g., image and reputation in the marketplace, goodwill, peace of mind, better on-the-job attitude from employees).

When it comes to leveraging, who in the organization would you target—Recommenders, Influencers, Decision Makers, or Approvers? Think of your best answer before you proceed.

. . .

This was a little bit of a trick question. You must be prepared to engage in leveraging with Approvers—which is the answer I bet you came up with. But . . . you must be ready to leverage with Decision Makers, too. Just like Approvers, they are interested in hard-dollar and soft-dollar value, and you must be willing to make your case to your sponsor *and* to the Approver who will be giving the final go-ahead on the sale. (You tell your sponsor everything, remember?)

Let me emphasize that you must be willing to articulate, with credibility and passion, both hard-dollar and soft-dollar value results in your discussions with Decision Makers and Approvers. Sometimes salespeople focus exclusively on one or the other, and that cuts down your effectiveness and opportunity.

Recently, I was presenting my own company's results to an Approver of a good-size office products company. In my attempt to leverage their desired results with my documented value, I said something like this:

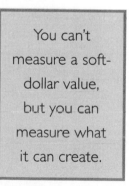

ME: "Mr. Approver, 15 percent of the one million alumni of my programs are in the office products industry, and they are reporting up to a 54 percent increase in entry point order size while at the same time cutting their sales cycles in half. They have become unstoppable in their attitude about selling and overperforming."

You can't measure a soft-dollar value, but you can measure what it can create.

At this point, the Approver looked up over his reading glasses at me and said, "Tell me more about their unstoppable attitudes."

TRANSLATION: "That hard-dollar stuff is interesting . . . but what I really want to hear about right now is soft-dollar value."

I immediately ditched the remaining hard-dollar value evidence I had prepared and started an entire conversation about the importance of employee attitudes, the lost opportunity organizations experience due to territories not being covered, and the fact that the competition has a way of winning over customers that were left unattended. None of these concerns could be documented by means of numbers, but all were of intense interest to my Approver.

He gave me the business and a reminder that, at some times and for some people, soft-dollar value is more appealing than hard-dollar value.

Referrals, case studies, and/or testimonials are powerful demonstrations of the social proof connected to the value that your organization has worked so hard to deliver. Be ready to discuss them—with passion and conviction.

These, then, are the four activities that match up correctly with the four hierarchy groups in your target organization. If you use them consistently and with the right people, you'll be in a better position to get, not just more second appointments, but more second appointments with the right people.

FROM COACH STEVE

Tony is challenging you to *think differently about your job as a salesperson* throughout this book. If you do the work necessary to adopt a different way of thinking, there will be a benefit that will serve not only your sales career but everything you attempt in life.

The benefit of practicing thinking differently is this: The more you practice thinking differently, the easier it becomes to embrace new and more productive ideas, approaches, and habits. And the better equipped you are to embrace new ways of doing things, the more effective you will be in outthinking, outsmarting, outworking, and outmaneuvering obstacles and competition on the road to success in everything you do.

Once you read this book, go through all the exercises, and write down all the stuff, you will have to hit the street and face the real world. And as you attempt to implement your newfound sales plan, there will be not less than a million unique circumstances that you will encounter that Tony didn't detail in this book. Now you could think, "Tony's book didn't tell me what I needed to know." But as your coach, I'm going to tell you flatly: *Everything you actually need really is in the book*. The single most important lesson Tony is teaching you by laying out these ideas the way he has is to *think differently*. Break from the habits, test new approaches, change old routines. If you do—you will be developing mental agility.

Think differently, become mentally agile, and learn—through Tony's example—to not be afraid of a little steeper climb. The view will be spectacular.

6

BUILDING A
FOUNDATION

In this chapter, you'll learn about the two critical foundation stones for setting more (and more productive) second appointments: effective visualization and the use of a tool I call the TIP sheet.

VISUALIZATION

Recently, I interviewed more than 100 CEOs, presidents, and owners of small, medium, and large organizations to find out what went into their success.

Along the way, I discovered that the most successful companies had processes for *everything:* finance, manufacturing, marketing, customer service . . . you name it. If it mattered to the organization, the most successful top bananas had figured out a way to turn it into a process.

A process is basically a recipe. It's the proven "what to do" and the reliable "when to do it" of what you plan to carry out. It's the ingredients and the sequence used to create any desired result. To craft a successful process, it's best to start with the end in mind and to state what you want as a positive picture for your mind's eye. For instance:

My goal is to get the second appointment and make the sale.

It makes sense to start developing our process with the end result in mind in this way. After all, if we want to build a six-story commercial building, we're not going to start by buying a piece of property that is zoned for a six-bedroom home.

And it makes just as much sense for us to state our desired end result in a positive way. This is because the human mind focuses powerfully on whatever we give it, *even when what we focus on contradicts the logical sense of what we think we are asking our minds to do.* For example, if I tell my mind, "I really don't want to be late for the meeting," guess what outcome my brain is most likely to fixate on? Being late for the meeting. That's what will come back to me. If, on the other hand, I say to myself, "I know I can figure out a way to be on time for the meeting," my mind fixates on the *desired* outcome. Phrasing commands and questions in a positive manner is extremely important in sales . . . and, indeed, in just about every aspect of life you can imagine.

Here's the payoff: I learned to my astonishment that the vast majority of successful individuals I was interviewing made a habit of *seeing* themselves being successful. They habitually *visualized* positive outcomes, as I've described and, as a result, they were much more likely to attain them.

You can understand, then, why I'm going to insist that you *see* yourself getting the second appointment and getting the sale. Such visualization is a very important part of the sales process.

Here's what a *positive* message might sound like before the beginning of your selling day:

I see myself making the best possible use of my time today. I see myself calling on suspects and prospects I believe to have a real application for my products, services, and solutions. By focusing on building and supporting relationships with the right people, I see myself setting, and making the most of, my first and second appointments with these prospects, and making the sale.

Take a moment and write your own positive message with regards to getting more second appointments and making the sale:

_____

_____

_____

_____

_____

THE ULTIMATE SALES TIP

Let's face it. To get the second appointment and make the sale, we
must first get the first appointment. And to get this initial meeting,
we need to prequalify the individual and/or enterprise that we're
going to make the first appointment with. This requires groundwork (sometimes referred to as "grunt" work). Once that work is
done, we'll have in place the first step in our sales process—the step
that will help us to ensure our desired end result.

Prequalifying is the most important phase of this groundwork.
I choose to prequalify every person, division, or location I contact
with a great degree of accuracy, and I think you should, too. Before
I pick up the telephone, drop in for an unannounced visit, or talk
to *anyone,* I make darn sure that the people I'm reaching out to fit
my criteria and are worthy of spending my time with. After all, I
have only eight hours to spend each selling day.

There are four areas of opportunity when it comes to prequalifying:

- Suspects.
- Prospects.
- Suspects in our existing accounts.
- Prospects in our existing accounts.

A *suspect* is any individual or enterprise who has not had any
proactive and/or direct contact with you or your organization.

A *prospect* is any individual or enterprise whom you have contacted or who has contacted you and who also represents a realistic

ntial for a near future sale. A *near future* sale is one that will
en in the sales year that you're currently selling in.

Prospects and suspects operate either within your existing
customer base or outside that base. The phrase *existing customer
base* describes any individual or enterprise that is currently
buying from you. The operative word here is *currently.* So anyone who is not buying from you now is, by default, either a
suspect outside your customer base or a *prospect* outside your
customer base.

Which of the people in these four groups should you reach
out to?

The answer lies in a tool I call the Template of Ideal Prospects
(TIP). This is, in essence, a tool that helps you to eliminate individuals and organizations that are likely to waste your time.

You know whom I mean: People who have neither the need nor
the resources (including the money) to buy from you.

Weeding out these folks early in the sales process is a habit I developed very early on in my sales career and one that I continue to
use to this day. This habit is one of the most important steps you
can take to ensure a higher total of meaningful second appointments . . . and a bigger commission check.

Here's how to develop your TIP. Grab your company's current
customer list. (Note that I didn't say to grab *your* customer list. We
want as many logos as possible.) You'll also need a notebook.

Once you've gathered these tools, head for the door. You're not
going out to make a sales call. You're bound for your home office,
the library, or some other spot that has the requisite quiet and a
business research department worthy of the name. These days, that
means high-speed Internet access.

TIP STEP ONE

Take a good, long look at that customer list you brought along.
Study all the customers very closely.

You may find that you need to break the list down into sub-
groups, industries, or niches. (For example, if your sales territory
or assignment is to sell to law firms and hospitals, separate those
industries into their own groups.)

TIP STEP TWO

Ask yourself the following question:

What do my company's best, biggest, and most profitable current customers have in common?

That question may seem breathtaking in its simplicity. It may seem like the kind of question you can answer with an "I know 'em when I see 'em" response. Don't fall into that trap. Give the best, fullest, and most detailed answer you possibly can. Record the answer in your notebook.

The attention and care you give to answering this question will determine the number and quality of second appointments you set . . . and the income you earn as a salesperson.

There's a reason for this. The longer the list of qualities shared by your company's best, biggest, and most profitable customers, the more accurately and completely you'll be able to prequalify your suspects and prospects.

A TIP EXAMPLE

Look at one of my actual TIP sheets (Table 6.1). I invite you to use it to develop a detailed, meaningful first draft of your own.

As a general—and very reliable—rule, I avoid making any substantial time commitment to anyone whose profile is even marginally different from the information I have taken the time to assemble on my TIP sheet for the questions numbered 1 through 9. I approach only companies that have nine of nine hits in this part of the sheet. (You can make a backup file for companies that hit *almost* all of your criteria, but I urge you to focus your initial efforts on only the perfect matches, especially if you're interested in making the sale in two calls.)

DON'T LEAVE HOME (OR YOUR OFFICE)
WITHOUT IT

Immediately after completing a visit to one of my existing customers, I pulled out one of my TIP forms, which I kept neatly organized in a portable file box in my trunk. (I prefer a low-tech, high-touch approach.) I decided to stop in unannounced so I could

TABLE 6.1   Template of ideal prospects.

Industry: Computer Hardware and Software Manufacturers

1. More than 150 salespeople:		Yes __X__	No _____	
2. Outsource sales training:		Yes __X__	No _____	
3. Complex sale:		Yes __X__	No _____	
4. Problem getting appointments:		Yes __X__	No _____	
5. Currently invest in sales training:		Yes __X__	No _____	
6. Use Internet for training:		Yes __X__	No _____	
7. Customer retention problems:		Yes __X__	No _____	
8. Prospect acquisition problems:		Yes __X__	No _____	
9. Sales cycles too long:		Yes __X__	No _____	

10. Titles of each player:			Names:
Recommender:		District Sales Manager	
	X	Area Sales Manager	Margaret Steven
		Regional Sales Manager	
		Salesperson	
Influencer:	X	Head of Sales Training	Jeanette Gabriel
		Sales Trainer	
		Chief Improvement Officer	
Decision Maker:	X	Vice President of Sales	Mel Silver
		Vice President of Marketing	
		Vice President of New Business	
Approver:	X	President	Johnie Casisa
		CEO	
		Owner	

drop off a card at the front desk of a nearby manufacturing company. It happened to have a perfect match on my TIP for manufacturing companies.

I walked the hundred yards or so to the lobby of Star Manufacturing from where I had parked my car. As I entered the building, I noticed pictures of telescopes and the night sky filled with little stars. It was a delightful space, quiet and softly lit, evoking the night sky in the pictures.

As I handed the receptionist my business card and my organization's most recent marketing slick (which at the time included a neat customer success story and case study), I said: "Could you please deliver this to Mr. Jacobs?"

The receptionist looked at my card with great interest and then looked at the front cover of what I handed her. She quickly flipped to the back cover and read its entire contents.

What she said took me completely by surprise: "I'll deliver this right now. Please wait here."

With that, she got up and walked through a door bearing an "Employees Only" sign. In a few short minutes, she returned and said, "Mr. Jacobs would like to see you. I'm his personal assistant. My name's Mary Ellen; please follow me."

I dutifully followed Mary Ellen into the inner workings of Star Manufacturing and made my way to Mr. Jacobs' corner office. As I walked into the office, I resisted all temptation to use an icebreaker statement and start blathering on about trivial points or about the huge family picture on the wall behind his desk.

Mr. Jacobs greeted me quickly and immediately asked me: "What's Hewlett Packard been up to?"

Wow! I gave a response about our entry into the manufacturing software arena and told him what we felt we had to offer the manufacturing marketplace. He actually listened to my rather long monologue. Then he slowly got up from his big leather chair and said three words: "Come with me."

For a moment, I thought I was about to be escorted out the front door and warned never to return. (I tend to look at the bright side of things . . . how about you?) But in fact, Mr. Jacobs was leading me on the brief journey to the office of the chief operations officer. It was a small, nicely appointed, well-organized space.

Mr. Jacobs made the introduction and quickly said: "Janet, I want you to find out if HP can help us out." Then he quietly walked out the door.

Janet and I spent the next hour and a half discussing the ins and outs of her operation. We set a date and time for our second appointment. As she walked me back to the lobby, she handed me her card. It read: Janet L. Jacobs, COO.

I asked: "Are you related to Mr. Jacobs?"

"Yes," she answered. "I am the oldest of his four daughters." (It came back to me then that the picture on the wall had shown Mr. Jacobs and five females, and I finally noticed the resemblance of Janet and Mary Ellen, Mr. Jacobs' assistant.)

"You should also know something else," she continued. "My father started our family business after a successful engineering career at Hewlett Packard in Palo Alto 15 years ago."

Good to know.

As I walked to my car, I said to myself: "Wow, what luck! What are the chances of that happening? Today's my lucky day!"

Actually, the more I prospected using my TIP sheets, the luckier I got. I went on to sell one of the largest computer systems in my long career at HP by using my TIP process.

That episode taught me a lesson, one that I refined over the years and went on to teach many, many salespeople at HP. It was a lesson about turning cold call visits into warm calls with top officers of companies. And it all started with developing a TIP.

Before you move on to the next chapter, create your own TIP. Make it detailed. Make it as specific as the sample TIP I shared with you. And then make a promise never again to phone, e-mail, or drop in unannounced on an individual or organization that does not represent a strong potential match for your products, services, and solutions.

LOCK IN WHAT YOU'VE LEARNED

I invite you to participate in an e-learning exercise that I've developed based on this chapter. Visit www.gettingthesecondappointment .com and click on Chapter 6 Online Assets. You'll get a chance to download a TIP form and see actual examples of various industry statistics.

7

PUTTING IT ALL TOGETHER

Warning: This chapter builds on what we covered in Chapters 1 through 6. If you came across this chapter while surfing through the book, you definitely won't want to drop in here until you've had the chance to assimilate the material covered in the earlier portion of the book.

WHAT WE KNOW FOR SURE

What do we know for sure so far? Well, among other things, we know:

- As sales professionals, we must guard the time we spend selling with a fair amount of jealousy.
- We're not going to spend any time with any individuals or organizations that are not a perfect fit to our TIP (see Chapter 6).

> Getting the second appointment with the right person will ensure that you make the sale in two calls.

To put it bluntly—we're not after just *any* old second appointment, but the *right* second appointment.

Now we're ready to take the next big step (which is actually four smaller steps) to get the second appointment and make the sale.

DEFINING THE SALES PROCESS

It's important to understand how long it takes you to sell whatever it is you're selling.

Sales process time is the total elapsed time it takes to move an individual or organization from the category of *suspect* (someone you want to turn into a customer) to the category of *customer*. If you've sold more than 10 customers or so, you already have enough experience under your belt to make a meaningful determination of your sales process time. (If you haven't sold this many customers, check with other salespeople in your organization or industry to get an idea of their history.)

Once you've determined this elapsed time, I suggest that you divide it into four components—exploring, initiating, sponsoring, and leveraging (see Chapter 5)—and determine how long you spend in each phase and what, specifically, you do in your sales process during that phase. Here's an example of my sales process time and the steps that constitute it:

Step One: Exploring (½ to 1 Week)

1. Complete my TIP (and identify my best prospects).
2. Survey over the telephone, via e-mail, or in person as many as five Recommenders within the organization and establish their most "profound pain."

Step Two: Initiating (1 to 2 Weeks)

3. Find out what's being done today to solve the pain—ask key questions that map my products, services, and solutions to the need. (We look at this questioning process in depth later in the book.)
4. Find out if the current way of addressing the pain is working and/or what any nonworking aspects might be costing the enterprise.

Step Three: Sponsoring (3 to 7 weeks; may overlap with Step Four)

5. Send the Decision Maker a profound piece of correspondence of introduction—a letter, an audio link, a CD, an e-presentation, a fax, a postcard, or a combination of these.
6. Call the Decision Maker to follow up. I leave a series of *polite, concise* voice-mail messages—one each week for seven weeks or until I receive a call back. (Everybody's got a unique selling environment, but you could do much worse than to follow my example.)
7. Create awareness and social proof, present my ideas, get sponsorship, present my agreement, and work out the terms and conditions.

Step Four: Leveraging (3 to 7 weeks; may overlap with Step Three)

8. Send the Approver an autographed copy of my best-selling book with one or more pages bookmarked.
9. Call the Approver to follow up. I leave a series of *polite, concise* voice-mail messages—one each week for seven weeks or until I receive a call back.
10. Get the approval to move ahead and begin our business relationship.

Take a moment *right now* to break down your sales process into steps and substeps. Do it on paper—not just in your head. Incorporate the four major steps—exploring, initiating, sponsoring, and leveraging—and include appropriate (and detailed) substeps within each of the main steps. Give a rough estimate for the amount of time you plan to spend in each step.

Use a notebook, a blank sheet of paper, or access the online resources for this chapter to develop a first draft of your sales process as I've laid it out here. Please *don't* turn the page and continue with this book until you've completed this written assignment.

> Four steps are all it takes to qualify and sell any prospect. However, they must be the right four steps.

• • •

YOUR CONSTANT IMPROVEMENT
CAMPAIGN (CIC)

Everything in the universe is changing and evolving; our sales process is no different. It's not standing still. It's either getting better and more effective or getting stagnant and less effective.

We have a responsibility to our career to commit ourselves to a Constant Improvement Campaign (CIC). We have to look for ideas to make whatever we use in our sales efforts work better. The possibilities we find for personal improvement can affect the results our product/service/solution delivers, our own careers, and, yes, our level of satisfaction and fulfillment with life itself.

To conduct an effective CIC, you have to be willing to experiment a little. Be willing to try something for its own sake. If it works, great; if not, try something else. Even if you come up with nothing at all or you identify a priority list of areas where you can take action to make things better, you'll be moving forward, not backward—and that's the whole idea.

Here are some specific ideas you can use to force the issue of constant improvement.

Analyze your sales process. The fastest way to analyze your sales process as to its overall effectiveness is to ask yourself three simple questions:

1. Does it take me too long to move someone from suspect to customer? If the answer is yes, how can I shorten the process?

Constant improvement never stops.

2. What substeps appear to be a waste of time? Which do I skip on a regular basis? (Hint: You should find a way to skip these all of the time.)

3. Which substeps have proven to be most successful? (Hint: You should find a way to spend more of your time doing these.)

Take control of your sales process. I'm not suggesting you attempt to run power trips during your meetings with prospects. I am suggesting that you take personal responsibility for ensuring that each step of your sales process is unfolding in a timely fashion. At the very least, you must know which step of the process you are in with any given prospect.

The essence of any process is that it is predictable and yields a certain result when followed. When any step of a process is forgotten or not completed on time, according to plan, the result changes. Establish the right plan, then follow it. By doing so, you maintain control.

Visualize your sales process. Most people tend to visualize important ideas and are motivated by pictures—and just about everyone *responds* to dramatic images. Unfortunately, however, with the advent of customer relationship management (CRM) and salesforce automation (SFA) software packages, the visual representation of sales goals has, in many organizations, taken a backseat to the number-driven, columns-and-rows of spreadsheet sales forecast.

Let's go back to the future for a moment and use the classic image of a funnel to represent the sales process (see Figure 7.1). This image enables you to see the number of suspects, prospects, and customers you're working on.

The basic concept behind the funnel metaphor is pretty simple: Given a constant flow into the top of the funnel (prospects), you'll get a constant flow from the bottom (customers/revenue/commission checks). Yeah!

You can elaborate on the metaphor, of course, if you try to put too much in at the top too quickly, it may spill over (meaning you

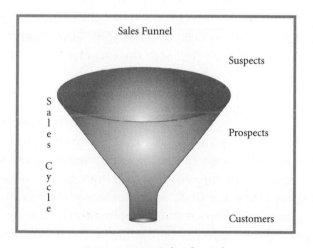

FIGURE 7.1   Sales funnel.

miss important steps, have too many calls to return, or develop more leads than you can follow up). If some "junk" gets stuck in the narrow part of the funnel (e.g., deadbeat prospects who take up too much of your time, demanding presentation after presentation and never making a decision), eventually, little or nothing will come out the bottom because of the unproductive and distracting blockage. You're so busy making presentations that everything else stops . . . and chaos begins (no customers/revenue/commission checks). Yuck!

A THING OF BEAUTY

A perfectly healthy sales funnel is a wonder to behold. It has just the right amount of suspects suspended over the top waiting to enter the process. In the middle section is the area that defines the actual steps that you need to take to make a suspect a customer. The more steps you complete, the closer your prospect gets to becoming a customer. And that's exactly what happens when they exit at the bottom of the funnel.

Exit, however, is a misleading word. It sounds so final. What about add-on business from your new customers? Those upgrades, new departments, locations, divisions, or other new selling opportunities show up again at the top as suspects and the whole beautiful process begins anew.

Let's look at the sales process we've been discussing in this book and place it *alongside* our classic sales funnel (see Figure 7.2).

TIME TO REVENUE

At the beginning of this chapter, I reminded you that you have to know how long it takes you to move an enterprise from prospect to customer. Take a moment now and divide your total sales cycle time into the three categories: initiating, sponsoring, and leveraging. We separate our funnel into these three groups of activities and omit exploring, the first step, because exploring is still an attempt to convert a suspect to a prospect, which is an out-of-the funnel activity. It doesn't fall within the sales process we're measuring here.

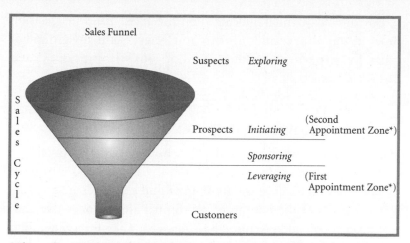

Sales Funnel

Suspects   *Exploring*

Prospects   *Initiating*   (Second Appointment Zone*)

Sponsoring

Leveraging   (First Appointment Zone*)

Customers

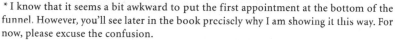

* I know that it seems a bit awkward to put the first appointment at the bottom of the funnel. However, you'll see later in the book precisely why I am showing it this way. For now, please excuse the confusion.

FIGURE 7.2   Classic sales funnel.

MANAGING YOUR PROCESS, NOT YOUR TIME

Many books, CD programs, software products, hardware products, seminars, and workshops are designed to teach salespeople time management skills. When all is said and done, the best time management system is one that's easiest for you to use and the one that works best for you.

It's not really possible to "manage" time. You can't tell it what to do, you can't change its direction, you can't speed it up, you can't slow it down, and you certainly can't save it. It simply passes, no matter what you and I do.

However, we can manage our sales process so that we can most effectively *use and invest* our time. I've identified three Success Steps that, when taken in the proper sequence, will move suspects into your funnel quickly and convert prospects to customers as fast as possible. To attain this worthy goal, you must manage your funnel process in the same way every day.

> You'll make bigger sales faster if you manage your sales process.

Day after day, you'll allocate time for each group in a certain order of importance and priority. You'll never skip any group because doing so will interrupt the flow of your sales process . . . and that's a definite no-no.

The Success Steps in order of priority follow.

PRIORITY ONE: REVENUE ACTIVITY

What do you see when you look at the bottom of your funnel?

At the bottom of my funnel, I see my highest risk prospects . . . the ones that I have the most time and resources invested in. The prospects at the bottom of my funnel are the ones I've educated, nurtured, and given my best ideas to. Therefore, these folks are (potentially, at least) easy pickings for my competition.

The bottom of the funnel, as we all know too well, is also where things can suddenly and mysteriously go wrong. Prospects can get cold feet, priorities can change, and opportunities can vaporize.

In addition, at the bottom of the sales funnel, sales managers have the most interest in "what's going on." Sales managers and other high-level types have a remarkable way of lining up four deep to partake in the glory activity of "picking up" the order . . . going for the "close."

> Prospects at the bottom of your funnel are prime targets for your competition. Set your appointment and make the sale today.

With everything that's going on, everything that's at stake, and all that visibility in our own organization, our first priority has to be to take all of the steps necessary to make the sale happen with each prospect in the bottom third of our sales funnel. We have to make turning these folks into customers and making sure their experience with our organization is superb our Job One.

Look at your own sales funnel right now. If you haven't yet populated the bottom third of your funnel with the names of real, live prospects, do so now before continuing with the book.

If you're not sure who should be in the bottom third of your funnel, use the following rules of thumb:

Bottom-third prospects are those who . . .

- You and your prospect have agreed to the terms and conditions of the sale.
- Your prospect has an approved budget.
- The Approver of the sale has agreed to the time frame to begin the business relationship. In other words, you're waiting for the ink to dry on your order.
- All that's left in the area of presale activities is for the Approver to have the contract signed.

Write down the names of all the bottom-third prospects in your funnel right now, before you continue.

• • •

PRIORITY TWO: CONVERSION ACTIVITY

Your next priority is converting suspects to prospects.

Skip the middle portion (for now) and perform the activities that will populate the *top* of your funnel.

There are at least two good reasons for managing your day in this way:

1. The very best time to perform the task of prospecting (i.e., moving suspects into your sales funnel) is just after you have made a sale. When you make the sale, you're pumped. Your conviction is running high. Your confidence is soaring. Rejection becomes an unfamiliar word reserved for less determined individuals than you. You are basically unstoppable at this point . . . so make the most of it.
2. Performing any other activity in your sales process would create a hole or empty area in your funnel.

> Working your sales funnel in the proper sequence will yield monthly, quarterly, and yearly sales performance in excess of your plan.

Whenever you skip or delay the activity of converting suspects to prospects, you are granting yourself permission to enter the hero/jerk continuum of sales performance. You're either the company hero or the company jerk. I warn you of this problem with, shall we say, ruthless compassion because I have myself experienced the continuum many times in my sales career. It's not much fun.

It goes like this: First, I win the salesperson of the quarter award, and during the very next quarter, I am on the brink of being put on probation.

No one—and I do mean no one—is perpetually immune to fear of professional or personal rejection. That's why it's normal to hate to prospect. But it's definitely *not* a good idea to avoid it. That's why converting suspects to prospects while we're in a good place (like making a sale) is so important and why I've placed prospecting so high on my priority list. I strongly suggest you do the same.

PRIORITY THREE: SPONSORSHIP ACTIVITY

Look at the middle of your sales funnel. This is where you will find the best prospects to move quickly into the bottom third. They may well be the people you've already had one meeting with—the people you're preparing for that all-important second meeting.

You've explored and initiated. Now it's time for sponsoring. This is where the real fun of selling begins: aligning your allies and getting your inside sales team to help you sell.

It's in strategizing with these folks (typically on second and subsequent meetings) that you get to use a critical sales tool: your advocacy lists.

Advocacy lists are scrupulously maintained contact lists that, by definition, are constantly in a state of flux. They contain the names, telephone numbers, physical addresses, and e-mail addresses for every sponsor you've encountered in your sales career. It's best to have four lists:

1. *The A list.* These are individuals you know in high places. They can be family members, friends, clergy, customers, and/or individuals that run the company you work for. My A list currently has 22 names of my biggest supporters. Some

are my friends, others are CEOs, and others are salespeople and alumni of my seminars. Don't ever forget or underestimate the power of the individuals who run the organization you work for. When is the last time you talked to your CEO or president? Do they know anyone in one or more of the organizations that you have in the middle third of your sales funnel? I bet they do.

2. *The B list.* These are individuals and/or organizations that have given you a referral during the current sales year. They're people you've followed up with. They can be suspects that have never bought from you—or long-standing customers. My current B list has more than 50 names on it. Do any of these folks know of someone (who knows someone who knows someone . . .) who can quickly be recruited as a sponsor of your efforts at the target organization? Find out. I bet they do.

3. *The C list.* These are all the board members (or equivalents) of my current customers. The most powerful name-drop you can use when looking for a sponsor is the name of a current or past board member or other high-level player. My current C list has more than 50 names on it. Take advantage of the people on this list—they have extraordinary networking skills and resources.

4. *The D list.* These are individuals in associations and groups that you belong to and are currently active in. My current D list has more than 100 names on it.

Make it easy to nurture your greatest supporters. Automate your advocacy lists!

Using any one or more of these lists can help you in quickly identifying someone (or a bunch of someones) as sponsors for each of the prospects that are in the middle third of your sales funnel. If you don't have any of these lists yet developed, your job of finding a sponsor won't be impossible—but it will be more difficult and more time consuming.

Take the time—keep track of your contacts and build the lists as you go along. It's definitely a wise investment of your time.

Follow those three steps every working day, tackle administrative and other duties once you've address the three priorities in the order I've given them, and I know you'll find that your time management problems take care of themselves.

I firmly believe that 75 percent of your sales activities will yield 125 percent of your quota performance . . . if (and only if) that 75 percent follow the guidelines discussed in this chapter. You'd be amazed (and perhaps amused) to learn how much work some salespeople do on activities that have little or nothing to do with moving the sales cycle forward.

LOCK IN WHAT YOU'VE LEARNED

I invite you to participate in an e-learning exercise that I've developed based on this chapter. Visit www.gettingthesecondappointment .com and click on Chapter 7 Online Assets. You'll get a chance to download a funnel form and see actual examples of other sales funnels.

8

THE FIVE DEADLY SINS OF APPOINTMENT SETTING

The following common sales errors fall into the category of *deadly sins* when it comes to getting the second (or, for that matter, the first) appointment. As you consider them—and, I hope, add them to your "not to do" list—think of how you feel when you encounter a salesperson who makes similar mistakes.

SIN NUMBER ONE: TALKING, NOT SPEAKING

There is a big difference between a salesperson who talks and one who speaks. Parrots talk. Babbling infants talk. Professional salespeople speak.

The major difference between talking and speaking is purpose. Salespeople must learn to speak about their products, services, and solutions with the prospect's purpose and result in mind. Talking means blathering on about what's on our agenda. If we want to get a second appointment, it is imperative that we never talk about anything.

Making a habit of talking rather than speaking can cost you the second appointment, the sale, and your sales career. On the other hand, speaking shows respect and honor for the other person.

Speaking intelligently, with the prospect's purposes in mind, is the sign of a confident, well-informed professional. If you want to get a second appointment, you must honor all aspects of your prospect's world. You must inquire about and truly understand the other person's objectives and speak with purpose.

To Avoid This Deadly Sin . . . Focus Your Communications

Before you write a piece of correspondence or pick up the telephone to make a call, you must have some understanding of the person you will be writing or talking to. What position does the person hold? What levels of influence and authority does he or she probably have? What typical challenges is this person likely to face? Asking these questions will help you focus on the purpose of your communications.

> Speak with your prospect's purpose in mind and they will buy from you. Talk to your prospect about your products, services, and solutions, and they will never grant you a second appointment or give you the sale.

Here are some tips to help you focus your communication:

- *Be very specific.* Choose a topic that is likely to make sense from your prospect's point of view, then make it crystal clear what that topic of discussion is at the outset of each interaction you have. You can do this diplomatically simply by giving your prospects a choice: "Would you like to discuss ideas to decrease the number of reworked assemblies, or is there something else that's a pressing issue at this time?"

- *Set a time frame for the first meeting, and you'll be more likely to get the second one.* Every prospect you come in contact with will appreciate your holding appointments to a certain time period. You'll focus in on a key prospect concern if you volunteer to play the role of sergeant at arms during all of your appointments: "We've agreed to keep our meeting this morning to 45 minutes. So, I've prepared an agenda for us—would you like to take a look at it before we get started?" "With only 15 minutes left, shall we address our next agenda item?" "Would you like to extend our allotted time by 30 minutes to cover the open items, or would you like to continue this conversation at some other time, say, this Friday at 3:00 P.M.?"

- *Be interesting.* I'm not suggesting that you present yourself as some kind of stand-up comedian, but I am suggesting that you speak in an engaging way. The best way for me to give you advice on this score is to strongly suggest that you join and participate in Toastmasters.

- *Be alert.* Every interaction you have with your prospects must be a learning experience. Fortunately, this is relatively easy. Prospects drop clues all the time as to how they want to be sold. Look for buying signals such as: "Would you be able to . . .", "Is it possible to . . .", "Do you charge for . . .", "I'd like my . . .", "Does it come in . . .", "How could we . . ."

SIN NUMBER TWO: USING BAD LANGUAGE

The fastest way to be shunted to someone other than the person you want to talk to—and to minimize the chance of getting a second appointment—is to use inappropriate language.

I'm not talking about foul language or jokes with adult content. (It should go without saying that that kind of communication is off limits.) Rather, I'm talking about using vocabulary that's unfamiliar to the person you're speaking with. This is a serious mistake that will immediately trigger a disconnect with the prospect, who is likely to feel as though you are out to intimidate him or her.

Whenever our prospects feel excluded or intimidated by technical terminology or other insider jargon, communication stops, the salesperson gets tuned out, and the appointment, for all intents

> No appointments, no callbacks, and no sales? Maybe you're talking the wrong words, instead of speaking the right language.

and purposes, is over. More often than not, the chance to return for a second meeting is lost. The people you're trying to build a relationship with will interrupt and say things such as: "I have people on my staff that handle these types of issues; I'll have my secretary connect you with them." In a heartbeat, you're shunted off to someone of a lesser influence and authority. (In more extreme cases, you may hear something like this: "I don't have time for this." Click . . . dial tone. And the conversation is over, forever.)

In general, the following rule applies when you communicate with people you want to sell to: You will be sent to the person you sound the most like. So make sure you use terminology that is familiar to your contact.

To Avoid This Major Sin . . . Learn Your Prospect's Language

Keep in mind that the purpose of any dialogue with your prospect is to understand his or her world. Therefore, you must learn to use the language and vocabulary of that world . . . not the language or technical jargon of the insular world many salespeople (especially salespeople who sell technical products) tend to live in. Remember that when you use one word that your prospect does not understand, you will trigger fear in that person, he or she will shut down, and your dialogue will turn into a monologue. You may think you have the person mesmerized by your eloquence . . . actually, you will have terrified him or her into silence.

To avoid such an outcome, find out what associations and professional groups your best prospects typically belong to. Then join those groups. Subscribe to their newsletter—and read it. Order recordings, transcripts, and minutes of the workshops and meetings they have at their conventions. As you peruse these documents and recordings, make note of the most common words these folks use to communicate. Then adopt and incorporate this kind of language into your dialogues with prospects. Also, when you're in your prospects' domains, notice what books they read. If you're not sure, ask. Once you find out, read them. Finally, make a list of at least 10 insider terms you use during interactions with prospects; then make a commitment to replace them with more prospect-friendly phrases or definitions.

The closer you can get to your ideal prospect's world, the easier you will find it to get first and second appointments.

SIN NUMBER THREE: MONOPOLIZING THE CONVERSATION

We all want to be heard. However, if you want to get the second appointment, you'll realize that monologues don't get second appointments, but dialogues do.

Monologues, by definition, are one-way communications. Monologues represent your own reality, a reality that tends to operate separately from the other person's opinions or needs. Getting the second appointment is all about understanding the other person's reality.

To Avoid This Major Sin . . . Give Yourself a Time Limit (And Stick to It)

During every interaction with any suspect or prospect, you must seek first to understand what's going on in the other person's world. Then and only then will your ideas be accepted and understood by contact.

The best way to do this is to set strict limits on your own talk time. Keep it under 60 seconds. You must never speak for more than 60 seconds without asking for approval to continue. This approval will come in the form of several types of questions.

> Reciprocity . . . you listen and when it's your time to speak, you'll be heard.

You can gain approval to continue for a fresh 60 seconds by asking *open-ended, prompting questions*. In general, these questions:

- Cannot be answered with a simple yes or no.
- Do not lead or control or try to manipulate the other person.
- Enable dialoging.
- Begin with the words *when, what, how, why,* or *where.*
- Require thought to be answered.
- Encourage the other person to reveal feelings.
- Build rapport.

The opposite of an open-ended question is a closed-ended question. *Closed-ended questions,* unlike the kind we've just examined, put an end to effective dialoging and will not get you any closer to a second appointment. Therefore, you should totally avoid this type of questioning as a means of getting approval to win another 60 seconds.

An example of a closed-ended question is, "You're interested in attracting new customers, right?"

The best place to use the closed-ended question is in a situation where you need to validate or confirm what you think is going on in your prospect's world.

In general, closed-ended questions:

- Are useful to give feedback during a dialog.
- Can be used to obtain specific information and/or confirm facts.

During a dialogue, if you need to make sure that you've heard the prospect correctly, you can use what's called a *clarifying question.* These questions, too, can win you a fresh 60 seconds. A good clarifying question might begin with the words, "So, if I understand you correctly, you're saying that . . ." (Warning: You should always preface your clarifying question with a statement such as this and then creatively paraphrase what you think your contact's main point is. It's a really bad idea to parrot back what you've just heard your prospect say. That approach may be perceived as condescending, sarcastic, and disrespectful.)

In general, clarifying questions:

> Too many closed-ended questions will close your conversation.

- Secure the other person's approval and prove to a greater degree that you have a good understanding of what they said.
- Express in your own words what you just heard.
- Clear up differences in the definition of words and phrases being used.
- Clarify the meaning of global words (such as *always* and *never*).

Typically, after you clarify with your prospect, you can use a *developmental question* to move the dialog in a desired direction to further understand prospects' purpose and/or result that they want to achieve. These questions, too, can win you another 60 seconds of time to talk . . . once the contact has responded to your question. In general, developmental questions:

- Encourage other people to elaborate on what they just said.
- Begin to make it possible for other people to show their true feelings about the topic at hand.
- Obtain further definition of what's under discussion.

Optionally, you can also use a *directional question* to win another 60 seconds. These questions steer the dialog to a certain direction that a developmental question just uncovered. Directional questions are like a road map of your conversation and allow the dialog to take another path, one that's beneficial to uncovering the prospect's purpose and needs. In general, directional questions:

- Move the dialog from one logical topic to another.
- Invite the other person to participate in an informational exchange.
- Can be used to replace a closed-ended question you were tempted to ask.

Important: Don't fall into the trap of using directional questions to control or manipulate the prospect in any way. This will destroy any business rapport you've built and reduce your chances of getting a second appointment.

Another question type you can use to earn another 60 seconds of talk time is called an *opinion question.* This kind of question is extremely helpful in revealing where a prospect stands on any particular issue, and it can be used to give you more insight into someone's unique needs. Opinion questions are also a nonthreatening way to ensure that the other person is actually engaged in the dialog. As a general rule, opinion questions:

- Ask a direct question in a nonconfrontational way.
- Get the other person to speak frankly and openly.

- Allow the opportunity to share feelings.
- Show esteem and respect for the other person.
- Help to extend and prolong dialogues.

Caution! Using a directional question incorrectly can actually move your prospect away from you and the sale.

Finally, you can use what I call a *social proof question* to justify another 60 seconds of talk time. This is an indirect way of getting other people to realize that their situation is similar to that of other people you've worked with. As with any other reference to a third party, there is the chance that your contact will respond favorably to what you cite within the question—on the other hand, there is a chance that the social proof you introduce will be looked on as competitive or irrelevant to what's being discussed. So these questions can be tricky.

In general, social proof questions:

- Introduce a third party that is relevant to the discussion.
- May increase confidence that you can address the purpose and needs of the other person.
- Validate the other person's reasoning.
- Can be used to address concerns or problems before they arise.

Intelligent use of each of these question types will encourage your prospects to begin to show their true feelings about whatever subject is under discussion and will build business rapport between you and your prospects.

SIN NUMBER FOUR: STRETCHING THE TRUTH

The "bigger is always better" mind-set will do your cause more harm than good. Exaggerating capabilities is an all-too-common practice. So-called little white lies fall into this category as well. Overpromising and underdelivering have an unfortunate way of coming back to haunt you—and sabotage your sale. So don't do it.

Face it. If you lie to yourself, you'll find it easier to lie to someone else. We must be willing to be totally honest and stand behind and deliver every word we say or write and every commitment we make—and we have to start by being truthful with ourselves. It's like adopting a culture; it becomes ingrained in everything we do, say, and how we act. We must become known for honesty and integrity.

> If being totally honest with your prospect costs you the sale, find something else to sell. And, someone else to sell for.

Applying the Golden Rule: Check Your Promises Closely

If you ever find yourself saying, "Let me be honest with you" or "To be perfectly honest . . ." (as though these were exceptional occurrences), guess what? You're due for a truth check-up.

Start by looking at every single piece of documentation you're currently giving to your prospects. Look at every piece of correspondence in your files. Is each completely accurate? Are you willing to stand behind each one? If not, change them.

SIN NUMBER FIVE: BEING A SPACE INVADER

Jumping into your prospect's space without being invited to do so is a great way to cut down on your second appointment totals.

I've gone on many sales calls with one or more business partners, and I can't count the number of times I've watched in horror as my colleagues placed papers, briefcases, notepads, or other materials on the prospect's desk without asking. That's the business equivalent of putting your feet on someone's coffee table.

Someone's office is like a home or automobile that doesn't belong to you. It is to be respected in accordance with the culture and habits of the other person. If you want to increase your chances of getting a second appointment, make sure that you honor your prospect's personal space during the first (and, for that matter, all subsequent) appointments.

For a moment, imagine there's an invisible 18-inch barrier surrounding your body. You probably don't have to imagine too much because there almost certainly is an invisible 18-inch barrier around your body. This is your *confidential* zone. This is the area most people hold as essentially private, a space to be occupied only by a spouse, a significant other, close relatives (children, for instance), and domestic pets (pythons excluded).

Barreling thoughtlessly into another's personal zone is tantamount to a physical challenge. So don't go barging in heedlessly. Cultural and regional differences may need to be taken into account here, so it's important to follow the other person's lead.

There *are* three other zones that you should be aware of:

- The *individual* zone between 18 and 32 inches from your body is where most of us are comfortable with social or business interaction that involves people we know.
- The zone between 32 and 44 inches from your body represents the *sociable* zone. It's about the distance between you and your prospect when you're sitting on a chair placed in front of the prospect's desk. In this zone, most of us are comfortable interacting with people we do not yet know well in social and business situations.
- Finally, the region outside these zones, known as the *common* zone, is the area where we are comfortable with (or at least occasionally prepared to accept) announcements of unexpected entrances from others.

To Avoid This Major Sin . . . Ask Permission, and Breach the Zones One at a Time

To honor the prospect's space, we must always ask for permission before making the transition from the common zone, to the sociable zone, to the individual zone, and, on very rare occasions, the confidential zone. By doing this, you'll be sending a message that you're respectful of the other person's belongings and physical boundaries. This message is critically important to gaining trust, building business rapport, and making the sale.

When you show up for an in-person appointment, stand at the threshold of your prospect's office and say something like "May I come in?" (Now you're in the sociable zone.) After you've been invited to sit down, do so, in the spot the other person indicates. (Now you're in the individual zone.) After a period of getting acquainted, you must ask for permission before you place any material on the prospect's desk.

You must enter the zones one at a time. It's a good idea to reserve moving into the confidential zone only if the other person invites you to do so. You can encourage your prospect to invite you into the various zones . . . but be careful. For example, if you must use a dry erase board or chalkboard, you might ask the prospect to join you at the board. Give the prospect a marker or piece of chalk; this brief point of contact within the person's confidential zone will help to encourage him or her to open up and participate.

LOCK IN WHAT YOU'VE LEARNED

I encourage you to access the Online Assets for all the relevant chapters before you continue. That way, you'll be able to practice what you've learned and build up some momentum before you move on. I invite you to visit www.gettingthesecondappointment .com. While you're there, take full advantage of your free trial membership in my special Getting the Second Appointment Success Portal.

9

POINTS OF ENTRY

W ho's the best person to make your first appointment with? As you sit in your office, cubicle, or other personal workspace, staring at the telephone or perhaps at your contact manager screen, you ponder the nominees: Recommender, Influencer, Decision Maker, or Approver. Before you make your decision and plot your contact strategy, *realize how important this decision really is,* and consider the following principle closely:

> *The* first *action you take in the relationship will have the* greatest *impact on (1) whether you get the second appointment and (2) whether you close the sale.*

Now, I know that's probably a controversial statement for many sales professionals. Let me explain why I feel qualified to make it.

I've been selling for 28 years. I've had hundreds of conversations on this topic, written dozens of articles for magazines about it, and given more than 750 speeches and seminars on the subject. And in addition to the principle I just outlined, there's one thing about prospecting I know for sure: You, my friend, are the only person who can eventually pick your target and take the action, write the letter, make the call, and show up for the appointment. You will decide to reach out to companies however you feel it is best to do so.

> If you make your first call on Approvers, they'll tell you where to go.

And you will make that decision many, many times over the course of a given selling year. What I want to do here is give you options. I will never challenge the fact that you have the right (and the privilege) to do it your way. All I ask is that you consider all the options before you make that choice.

What I unfold in this chapter will give you the tools necessary to make the right decisions and then to make the most out of all the contacts you do make—regardless of the person you decide to reach out to. At the end of this chapter, I share the way that I "do it" in my sales process. You may choose to follow my example, or you may not. But whatever road you take, please remember that, in my experience, the group or person within the target organization that you choose to reach out to first, and the *way* you choose to reach out to that group or person, will have a profound effect on your outcome with that target company.

INTERACTING WITH THE RECOMMENDER

As you recall, the role of the Recommender is, as the name implies, to provide an opinion and/or to make a recommendation in a certain area or activity.

I've already warned you to avoid making any attempt to "sell" a Recommender, whether on the phone, in person, via e-mail, or by any other method because these people are not empowered to buy.

Attempting to sell to a Recommender is like trying to teach a pig to climb a ladder. You'll get extremely frustrated in the process—and you'll only get the pig mad. As I mentioned earlier in the book, you'll be *exploring* with the Recommender (typically, but not always, by phone). In doing so, you'll want to keep the following tips in mind:

Key Winning Results for the Recommender
- Feeling helpful.
- Being more popular.
- Getting attention.
- Being confided in.
- Becoming a friend.

- Having an easier process to work with.
- Having more free time.
- Being able to brainstorm.
- Feeling a part of the team.
- Doing what's right for everyone.
- Never ruffling the feathers.
- Seeing things get done.
- Having the Recommender's ideas matter.

Rules of Engagement for Interacting with Recommenders

1. *Don't* ask them to buy anything.
2. *Don't* ask them to make any decisions.
3. *Do* ask them questions about whatever they are using today that you hope to *replace* with your products, services, and solutions.
4. *Do* ask them how they feel about their current situation as it applies to your products, services, and solutions.
5. *Do* ask them for their advice.

WHEN POSING QUESTIONS TO A RECOMMENDER

Remember that all of your dialogs with the Recommender should have the look and feel of a friendly conversation. These conversations must never come off sounding like an interview, interrogation for confidential information, negotiation, or sales pitch.

Consider asking the Recommender questions such as:

- If you were I, how would you approach [your vice president of sales and marketing]?
- What's the most difficult part of your job? What about your job is causing you the most frustration right now?
- When your [printer] stops working, what sort of problems does that cause you?
- Who else is affected when this takes place?
- If you had [two more hours] each day, how would you spend them?
- If you could change anything about your [network], what would that be?

- What are the top [three] areas in your department that you feel need the most improvement?
- Who does your [manager] report to?
- Who normally presents your ideas to [top management]?
- How long does it take to get [a decision] made in your department?

Write your ideas here:

_____

_____

_____

_____

INTERACTING WITH THE INFLUENCER

You'll recall the role of the Influencer is to be the trusted advisor of the Decision Maker(s). These people pass on their personal and professional judgment on the tactical components of what the Decision Makers need to get accomplished for the Approver.

Let's say that, for whatever reason, you decide to make your first telephone call to an Influencer. Or perhaps you're out in your territory cold calling, you drop in to make a person-to-person call, and you find yourself face to face with an Influencer. Or maybe an Influencer called to invite you to a meeting. (I have always found it interesting that when I've been asked to give a presentation to an Influencer, it's always best to be prepared for *more* than the expected number of Influencers I've been told will attend. Influencers seem to be like hangers in the closet . . . they multiply while you're not looking.)

Keep in mind that Influencers love to dive head first into oceans of facts, figures, charts, comparisons, demonstrations, analyses, and endlessly comparing one of these elements to some other one. They love doing this because splashing around in all the pie charts and spreadsheets helps them to do one of three things:

1. Prove their technical expertise.
2. Find "evidence" to back up their (almost always negative) first impressions.

3. Or, if you're really lucky, establish the viability of what you have to offer.

(*Warning:* Outcome 3 is pretty rare on any first-call situation, which is why I personally don't like dealing with Influencers.)

KEY WINNING RESULTS FOR THE INFLUENCER

If you want to be a hero in the eyes of Influencers, you must focus on *all* of the following results:

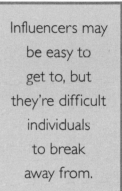

Influencers may be easy to get to, but they're difficult individuals to break away from.

- Getting it right the first time.
- Helping them build their empire.
- Help them be seen as the ultimate problem solver.
- Letting Influencers feel they are in control.
- Honoring their personal rulebook.
- Doing what they say.
- Doing what they say on time.
- Giving them all the credit.

Rules of Engagement for Interacting with Influencers

1. *Don't* get defensive if they question your product's capabilities, the merit of your ideas, or your personal ability to deliver anything.
2. *Don't* use numbers and percentages to make your case unless they are 100 percent accurate, verifiable, and defendable. When in doubt, understate (so you can eventually overdeliver).
3. *Don't* interrupt Influencers when they are speaking for any reason whatsoever. If you fail to observe this rule, you will prove to the Influencer that you don't really know or care about the situation he or she faces. Interrupting *anyone* is usually a bad idea, but it's a particularly disastrous gambit when you're dealing with Influencers.
4. *Do* be as detailed as possible.
5. *Do* be as accurate as possible.
6. *Do* be totally honest . . . don't stretch the truth, especially when it comes to discussions of your product's capabilities.

7. *Do* help the Influencer clarify his or her priorities for you. (Use developmental and opinion questions to do this; see Chapter 8.)

8. *Do* appeal, where appropriate, to the endorsements of authoritative third parties that this Recommender would easily recognize and (more importantly) respect.

9. *Do* stay very narrowly focused. This is a major challenge for most of us salespeople.

> Don't ask your Influencer "Who's who?" It's a one-way street to being pigeonholed.

10. *Do* use only your current products, services, and solutions as a starting point. Never present future releases or upgrades that are "in the wings" or "almost ready for release." Sell only what's on your price list. Sell only the solution you know you can deliver.

11. *Do* resolve one issue before proceeding to the next. Influencers will not be interested in focusing on the issues you raise until they are convinced that you are following the correct logical sequence (namely, theirs).

WHEN POSING QUESTIONS TO AN INFLUENCER

Consider asking questions such as:

- Is there any special place that you would like to begin this [discussion/conversation/discovery/evaluation/qualification/elimination process . . .]?
- How would you like this [automated slicing machine] to work for you?
- What information would you like to have?
- What are the four most important characteristics you're looking for in your new [office furniture]?
- All right, [quality, guarantee, steel frames, and cherry wood] were at the top of your list. How do these requirements compare to your existing [office furniture]?
- What don't you like about the way your current [office furniture layout] affects [traffic patterns] in your department?

- If you could do it all over again without any restrictions, what would your new [accounting system] look like?

Important note: Because seemingly trivial communication choices can have long-lasting positive (or negative) impact during conversations with Influencers, I'm passing along the following important list of *do* and *don't* utterances. Review it closely before any discussion with one of these folks.

DO say:
- We are certain . . .
- We've confirmed all the information . . .
- Our research team has located . . .
- X perfectly matches the capabilities of Y. (But say this only if you can prove it.)
- I've personally confirmed . . . (But use this only after you have earned the right to say so.)

DON'T say:
- How can I help you to . . . ?
- This will help you better understand . . .
- Do you need help with. . . . ?
- It appears that you need help in . . .
- Maybe we can get you in to see one of my other customer's sites. (Influencers know that their world is unlike anyone else's.)
- We have about 75 other customers that use this [forklift].
- I don't know . . .
- There's no way to prove . . .
- We can't do that . . .
- I'm not sure, but . . .
- Can I ask for your help?
- I'm confused . . .
- Would you take just a moment and help clear something up for me?

> Remove the word *try* from your vocabulary. Either you can or you can't.

- It's a gamble but I am pretty sure it will work . . . (or any variation).
- I'll try to find out . . .
- I'll try to get it to you by . . .

(Do not use any phrase containing the word *try*. Influencers are a little like Yoda—for them, there is no *try*. Either *do*—or *do not*.)

Write your ideas here:

INTERACTING WITH THE DECISION MAKER

The role of the Decision Maker, as we've seen, is to identify and sponsor the tactical initiatives that will overaccomplish the strategic initiative of the Approver—and to do this very quickly.

Time to implementation is always a key factor in the world of the Decision Maker. A couple of key words when interacting with these folks are *trust* and *recognition*. Another important point to bear in mind when working with Decision Makers: If you knowingly and willingly recruit a Decision Maker (you know, that past loyal customer at Old Company who is now working at New Company) and you then go over his or her head, you will kill your sale . . . no ifs, ands, or buts.

> Decision Makers are tactical thinkers and great talkers. Who else does that sound like?

Decision Makers are like racehorses. It's not practical to change them in the middle of the race. Remember, this person is your sponsor, supporter, cheerleader, confidant, advisor, and mentor and must be treated as such. Tell him or her *everything*, and make sure this person knows and approves of what you intend to do, before you do it.

Key Winning Results for the Decision Maker

- Being seen (by you and everyone else in the organization) as *the* team leader/player.

- Being seen (by you and everyone else in the organization) as the ultimate mentor/advisor.
- Getting everything done on time and under budget.
- Getting a promotion.
- Being upwardly mobile.
- Getting recognition (and perks) from the Approver.

Rules of Engagement When Interacting with the Decision Maker

1. *Don't* challenge the opinions and/or advice of your Decision Maker(s).
2. *Do* keep your topics to tactical issues.
3. *Do* let the Decision Maker do most of the talking. You'll learn more that way, and you'll win points for being an interested person.
4. *Do* keep your conversations uncluttered and free of too many details. Stay at the 30,000-foot level with your Decision Maker. Thumbnail sketches work best.
5. *Do* focus on exchanges that involve reactions, feelings, and responses.
6. *Do* make brief, credible, and sincere compliments. (Stature and acknowledgment are very important to the Decision Maker.)
7. *Do* listen carefully. Decision Makers tend to build alliances with people who have good listening skills.

WHEN POSING QUESTIONS TO A DECISION MAKER

Consider asking questions such as:

- May I ask you . . . If you were I . . . How would you approach your organization to sell them [wireless network services]?
- What areas of common ground (or common interest) do you see between our two organizations?
- What sort of ideas can we come up with that would benefit both of us?
- How do you feel about what is being accomplished so far and what still needs to be done?

- How do you feel about your organization's direction to-ward . . . ?
- You're my first priority; I'll do whatever I need for us to . . .
- Will you be in a position to [move forward/start up/initiate/resolve/tackle] these issues before the end of this [week/month/quarter/year]?

> You have found the mother lode when one of your Decision Makers moves to a new company in your territory that fits your TIP.

- Can we keep this just between you and me?
- Everyone speaks highly of our [spare parts policies]—what are your thoughts?
- This issue seems to be of concern for your [marketing department]; what do you think?
- What's been keeping you awake at night concerning your [year-end plans]?
- Could you paint your perfect scenario of how this would work out?
- I can get my [service department] to do it just this one time.
- We'll do [it] only for you.
- One of your organization's strategic initiatives was to [capture the European market]. How did that go? What remains to be done?
- What obstacles do you think we'll face that may be serious for you?

By the way, using *any* sentences and phrases that include the words *can't, shouldn't,* and *don't* is likely to lead to problems during your interactions with Decision Makers. You should be ready to pull out all the stops for your sponsor—and avoid the following phrases or any variations on them:

- We can't. . . .
- We can do [this/that] only for our major clients. . . .
- That's not available. . . .
- I can't get my company to do. . . .
- Your organization doesn't qualify for. . . .
- I can only. . . .
- That's outside my area of responsibility.

Write your ideas here:

_____

_____

_____

_____

Finally, if you have a Decision Maker from one of your past customers at Old Company who is now in a position of authority at New Company, you should consider saying something like this:

If you and I could redo what we accomplished at Old Company, what would you do differently?

And now, a true story . . . There I was, on my first sales call at the largest copier manufacturer in the world. I was standing in the conference room waiting for the vice president of sales. He walked into the room and smiled at me.

"I'm Bill McDermott," he said. "Thanks for coming to see me." His cheerful and energetic voice matched his firm but friendly handshake. He immediately handed me his card. As I took it, I held it at arm's length and said: "Bill, what's interesting about your card is that if you hold it right here and turn it ever so slightly, all you see is the word *president* under your name."

Two-thirds of Approvers were once salespeople.

A huge grin spread over his face. He leaned toward me and said in a low, almost conspiratorial tone: "It's funny that you say that, Tony; it's my personal goal to be the youngest president here at my company."

My response was immediate: "I'd love to help you do it!"

Within the first year of our business relationship, he became the youngest divisional president—and the greatest sponsor of my products, services, and solutions at that organization. Today, he is the CEO of one of the largest software companies in the world. And we still keep in touch.

The moral of this (true) story is that you must always be working toward understanding what your Decision Maker's goals are. That's one of the most important jobs a salesperson has.

INTERACTING WITH THE APPROVER

In every sale, there will always be an Approver whose job is to do just what the name implies. These folks, as I hope you remember, approve—or reject—whatever initiatives are being proposed and whatever purchases are being contemplated.

The Approver is the most important customer you'll ever have. When approval happens, a sale is made . . . and not a minute sooner.

The Approver may be an individual acting on his or her own behalf; think of the owner of a small company or the head of a household. Alternatively, the Approver may be a group of people acting on the behalf of an individual; think of a board of directors approving the recommendations of a CEO or president.

To master the art of getting the second appointment and making the sale in two calls, you must find, qualify, and sell the Approver. The best way to begin this process is to remember that Approvers *know* they are sitting at the top. They *know* they have the ultimate veto power. Their job is to have the vision and mission of the organization well in place and understood by all whose job it is to make that happen. Therefore, when we purposefully put ourselves in front of these all-important individuals, we must keep in mind that they have big egos, power, and control . . . and we must always bear in mind that authority is extremely important to them.

Approvers are brief, direct, and to the point. They spend a good part of their day making decisions. They think in terms of the big picture. They are fast movers. Image is important to them. They are not just low on patience—they have *no* patience. And they are highly competitive and are far beyond motivation. They are indeed driven to succeed.

Here's a reality check for you. Take the time right now to reread the previous paragraph. As you do, take a pencil and underline the traits of the Approver that you have in common. Please don't proceed with the rest of this chapter until you've finished this exercise.

• • •

What did you find out? If you're like most of the salespeople who attend my seminars, you just found out that you have many, if not all, of the same traits as the Approver.

That means that of all the individuals you'll meet in your suspect's, prospect's, and customer's world, you'll need to be the most careful when interacting with this person because people with similar working or personality styles do not necessarily get along or work well together. In fact, they may even rub each other the wrong way.

To work well with the Approver, you'll have to check your ego at the door and learn to keep your talk time to an absolute minimum. Why? Because, the quickest way to totally turn off the only person who can say no to you when everyone else is saying yes is to challenge the Approver's ego, power, control, and authority. And that's all too easy to do. Remember, the person who is doing all of the talking has the implied power and authority and that should not be you.

Sadly, you can challenge the Approver even without meaning to—by triggering either of the two very real fears that they have. (Yes, individuals at the top have fears, just as you and I do!) As a matter of fact, it's been my personal experience that when you *avoid* triggering the following fears, you'll be well on your way to building a good relationship with the Approver of your sale.

Fear Number One: Wasting Time

Every Approver I've ever met has lived in a time-compressed world. Everything in the Approver's world is measured against the denominator of time.

You can bet that whenever you're in a conversation with an Approver, whether on the telephone or in person, your contact will be either looking at a watch or thinking silently: "How much longer will this take?" This time obsession, as it applies to discussions with salespeople, is attributable to two factors. First, the salespeople who have come before you have proven to the Approver that discussions with salespeople can be a waste of time. Second, the Approver tends to feel that he or she doesn't get enough done during the course of a day and will deflect this feeling on to whichever unfortunate person happens to sit down with him or her. There's

> How many of the key results that Approvers look for can you deliver?

not much you can do about the second problem, but you can begin to make some headway with the first problem by keeping your conversations and meetings brief and to the point—and delivering what you promise.

Fear Number Two: Engaging in Conversations That Contain Unfamiliar Words and Phrases

Approvers, as we've seen, have huge egos, and they're not always good at asking for explanations of things they don't understand. As a result, they are *fearful of salespeople who use unfamiliar words and phrases.*

Engaging in conversations that contain such words and phrases will not only cause a disconnect between the salesperson and the Approver, but also automatically trigger fear number one! Now, that's what I call a "lose-lose."

Identify those terms you use that are likely to intimidate Approvers, and avoid those terms at all costs. Learn the language of your Approvers, and focus on the words and phrases they use most and understand most easily.

I am not suggesting that you prepare for your interactions with the Approver(s) of your sale preoccupied with either of these fears. I do, however, strongly recommend that you focus like a laser beam on the *purpose* of your communications with the Approver, and avoid all potentially troublesome words and phrases. Doing so will help you stay on the message and avoid triggering either of these fears.

Key Winning Results for the Approver
- Increasing shareholder value.
- Keeping stockholders happy.
- Overachievement of anything and everything.
- Underbudget performance of anything and everything.
- Increasing effectiveness.
- Increased efficiencies.
- Beating the competition.
- Holding on to existing customers.
- Getting add-on business from those customers.
- Cutting nonvalue expenses.

Did you notice the profound difference in the list of Key Winning Results of the Approver as compared to those of the people in the enterprise? The results of the Approver are all organization-focused, not me-focused. Why is that? Because the Approver *is* the organization. Whenever you address the overachievement of the strategic initiatives of the enterprise, you are automatically addressing the key winning results of the Approver *as an individual* . . . and that's a great place to be.

Rules of Engagement with the Approver

1. *Don't* challenge this person's ego, power control, or authority.
2. *Do* be as brief and to the point as they are.
3. *Do* keep your focus on their agenda.
4. *Do* give choices and let the Approver guide the conversation.
5. *Do* cut the industry jargon and technobabble from your vocabulary; use only words familiar to the Approver.
6. *Do* keep your talk time to less than 10 seconds at a time. (With everyone else in the organization, the standard is 60 seconds; with the Approver, it's 10 seconds.)

WHEN POSING QUESTIONS TO AN APPROVER

Consider asking questions such as:

- What specific goals, plans, and objectives do you have between now and the end of this [month, quarter, fiscal year]?
- Are you looking for an idea to eliminate any unintentional inefficiencies in your [name of] department/division?
- What's important to you personally about [mention one of this Approver's goals, plans, or objectives]?
- What are your personal expectations of a [business partner/provider/solutions provider/supplier] that can help you solve your [mention one of this Approver's goals, plans, and/or objective] during the next [month, quarter, fiscal year]?
- If we can sustain exceeding your expectations and solve your organization's requirements,

> Making the sale in two calls demands that you start your sales process at the top.

could you see yourself becoming one of our [customers/ clients] by the end of this [month/quarter/fiscal year]?

Write your ideas here:

_____

_____

_____

_____

THE BEST CALL YOU CAN MAKE

For us to firmly plant ourselves in the best possible opposition and quickly make the sale, consider the answer to the perennial sales question, "Who's the best person in the organization to contact first?" The following sequences are the way I perform my own sales process and target each of the categories in the enterprise.

First and Foremost

Qualify the enterprise by making a sales call on the Approver. Leverage your knowledge of your niche with the goals, plans, and objectives of this enterprise. Establish a firm understanding of this Approver's business criteria and find out if any unshakable loyalty exists between this person and your most formidable competitors.

Then

Qualify the enterprise by exploring all the company data with the Recommender (or a bunch of Recommenders). Find out what's going on today and who's who in the organization/enterprise.

After That

Qualify the enterprise by initiating with the Influencer by understanding what the enterprise is using today and what it lacks in form, fit, and function. Look at the technical criteria required to exceed expectations and start the process of mapping your products, services, and solutions to the organization's perceived needs.

Finally

Qualify the enterprise by making a sales call on the Decision Maker. Plant yourself firmly and positively in the decision-making process by getting the Decision Maker to sponsor you and your ideas.

How would you like for us to spend the rest of our time together mastering the four steps I just outlined? Along the way, I'll teach you how to *get invited back* for the second appointment . . . and make the sale in record time. Sound like a plan?

FROM COACH STEVE

It's been a few chapters since we've sat down for a locker room chat. Because we are about at half time, let's take a look at where we are and how we are going to set up the second half for the final victory.

You probably picked up this book with a desire for a higher level of success in selling. Once you cracked the cover, Tony began guiding you very strategically through a new view of whom you are taking your sales efforts to. He has helped you set your focus and attitude in a successful direction. And he has gently challenged you to examine nonproductive habits or patterns in the way you communicate in the sales process.

So here are some tough questions for you. Are you answering all of Tony's challenges with justifications designed to protect the way you have always done things? Are you avoiding implementing any of his strategies on the theory that "He doesn't understand my selling situations"?

The deadly resistance-to-change disease always presents the symptoms of justification, excuses, and cynicism. And these reactions are usually so sudden as to seem automatic. We have to make a *conscious* effort to overcome them.

To be open to positive change, we have to admit that what we have been doing doesn't support our current goals.

Ouch!

(continued)

Am I saying that to change our results, we have to admit that we have wasted our time on things that didn't work?

Yep.

But don't worry. You are in good company. There is not a single peak performer in sales—or any other arena, for that matter—who hasn't made mistakes. Then—and this is critical—they made the quiet but profound confession that what they thought was a good idea before simply didn't work at the level it needed to. Only at that time were they equipped to begin fresh with a new, better way of reaching the top.

So, if you haven't already, let go of the resistance that will keep you stuck and stale in the habits and thinking that you know you aren't satisfied with. Save the energy you might otherwise use on justification and excuses and instead *implement everything Tony is suggesting*.

Review the first half of the book to see what good ideas you may have overlooked or found reasons not to implement. Decide how you're going to put them into practice. Then get ready to pull out all the stops in the second half.

10

10 Principles for Delivering More Second Appointments

Here's my list of nine *simple* things you can do and one not so simple step you can take to increase your odds of scheduling more (and more productive) second appointments.

1. *Never make your first sales call into the account with an individual who's positioned too low* . . . and thus couldn't make a decision to buy your stuff even if he or she liked it. I call this common error "getting pigeonholed." Pigeonholed means getting stuck in one or a series of small compartments that restrict motion and movement and limit activities.

2. *Never ask other individuals to sell for you.* This common mistake happens whenever you agree to a prospect's statement that sounds like this: "I'll take your proposal and get it approved." If, at this point, you thank the person for his or her help, sit back, and relax, you should be prepared to kiss the sale goodbye. No one you encounter in the prospect's organization is going to be better at

selling what you sell than you are. Can you have sponsors? Sure. But there's a big difference building an alliance with someone else—and letting someone else sell for you. In the former case, you work *with* someone who has demonstrated both responsibility within the organization and an interest in working with you. In the latter case, your outlook is a lazy one; your strategy is basically reactive, meaning you sit back and wait for something interesting to land on your dinner plate. *Don't expect—or allow—someone else to do for you what you need to do for yourself.*

3. *Never overeducate the prospect about the product.* Somewhere along the line in our sales training, someone seems to have taught all of us that our job is to fill the prospect in on *all* aspects of what we sell . . . to provide so much information that the person could not possibly have any doubt about how our product, service, or solution is delivered or how to use it. Guess what? There is a difference between passing along information and delivering value. When we overeducate our prospects, we basically say, "I am first, last, and always a source of product information for my customers." If only it were so simple! Our customers demand more from us—our business sense, our knowledge of our own organization's capabilities, and our ability to listen to and persuade others in the prospect's organization, to name just three areas.

> Speaking to your prospect's needs can happen only after you've listened to their unique situations.

4. *Never make a prescription before you make a diagnosis.* If a doctor does this, it's malpractice. In sales, though, the same mistake is often mistaken for "competitive spirit." In both cases, the error can bring about disastrous complications. I've seen a good many sales opportunities go right down the porcelain fixture because the salesperson made costly—and inaccurate—assumptions about the prospect's needs. On or shortly after the first appointment, they think to themselves (or even say out loud), "Gee, this looks just like the Bradley account . . . what they need is . . ." That's sales malpractice. That's acting in ignorance and/or neglect of basic professional standards of care. Don't do it.

5. *Never present too soon.* For some reason, we salespeople think that sales are made only after a formal presentation is made. If we believe that statement is true, it stands to reason that the sooner we present, the sooner we'll make the sale, get the commission, and buy the toys that we want. Heck, why not make the presentation on the first meeting? (Answer: Because doing so may be a waste of everybody's time.)

6. *Never try to up-sell too soon.* If you're looking for a great way to extend an already long sales cycle, try adding on to the initial need before the initial need is satisfied. All too often we salespeople sell beyond the sale. That's a big mistake. Over the years, I've figured out that it's much easier to get a *customer* to buy something from me than to get a *prospect* to buy that same item. Why is that? Because once a commitment is made and the prospect becomes a customer, the playing field changes. It's all in the commitment and comfort level and the trust that commitment brings. Therefore, it's imperative that we *make the first sale as easy as possible.* Think simple configurations, minimal options, minimal cost, maximum value, and maximum return on investments. The bottom line: Avoid greed-based selling on the first appointment (or at any other point in the sales cycle).

7. *Never ignore objections or answer them incompletely.* You've heard this piece of selling advice as many times as I have: "Objections are a request for additional information." Why is it, then, that we salespeople take objections so personally? When we don't answer an objection, we instantly devalue our relationship with the other person. This degrades trust in the relationship and dramatically increases the likelihood that we will delay or derail the eventual buy decision. Any unanswered or glossed-over objection will put you on the fast track to nowhere. Any objection you choose to ignore, paper over, or otherwise deprive of your attention can be expected to spring to life and bite you, where you really don't want to be bitten, usually at the most inopportune moment imaginable.

8. *Create a sense of urgency.* If I had a $10 bill for every time I watched a salesperson enthusiastically agree to being fobbed off, sidetracked, or otherwise placed at the bottom of the contact's

priority list, I'd be a very rich man. Why are so many salespeople so willing to accept delay? Why do we agree to sit quietly and wait for the white or black smoke to come out of the chimney, like the faithful clustered in front of the Vatican when the College of Cardinals gathers to elect a Pope? Why do we have no other reply to "Call me back in three months" than something lame, like: "Okay, three months from now, let's see, how about 9:00 on the morning of the 16th of shall we say the month of 'never'?" Talk about encouraging a long, drawn-out, sales process! When your prospect puts you off and you instantly agree, you have a *no-sale* situation in the making. The passage of time has a profound negative effect on your sales message. In fact, it turns your message into a memory. Let's call this the *perched-pen* syndrome—it's the bad habit of settling for delay or resting in an unfavorable position.

Important Note: Whenever you get this put-off, say to whoever is doing the putting off: "Ms./Mr. Prospect, if you had to make your decision to [buy/invest/move forward/engage] with my company right now, what would your decision be?"

We know from previous chapters that Recommenders and Influencers can't buy anything. Therefore, this question can be asked only of the Decision Makers and/or Approvers. And if they are stalling, it's most likely for a good reason, and you'll most certainly find it out with this question.

9. *Always ask for referrals.* Most salespeople don't realize it, but *failing* to ask for the names of others you can talk to, either in the target organization or at other companies, is a major sales handicap. *Not* asking for an internal referral will make any new sale a more difficult one—because failing to ask prolongs the amount of time you spend in the undesirable category of *solicitor* (as opposed to *ally*) and makes it more likely for you to get pigeonholed. When a salesperson asks for a referral, he or she builds loyalty with the person giving the referral *and* jump-starts the sales process with the person being referred to. Getting referrals also means you spend less time on the phone with strangers, trying to talk them into meeting with you.

A caution note about internal referrals: Name-dropping within an enterprise is a powerful tactic if the name you happen to be dropping relates and resonates with the person you're dropping it on. Don't make the big mistake of thinking everyone is popular and respected. When in doubt, ratchet up to the next highest person until you reach a Decision Maker.

> Referrals are to salespeople as gold is to a miner.

A caution note about external referrals: Never use the name of a competitor of your prospect to gain audience. If the prospect just lost a deal or existing customer to their competitor, they'll wind up wanting to "shoot the messenger."

The previous nine principles for simplifying and streamlining your relationships with prospects are the easy things to change.

As it happens, though, there's one more principle that will deliver more and better second appointments. It's not quite so easy to implement. It's this principle that I want to share with you before we move on to the next chapter.

By now, you should have a pretty good idea what this principle is. However, as I've said before, I know I can't *force* you to initiate this routine when you reach out to people and organizations that fit your Template of Ideal Prospects. You, and you alone, must decide whether the effort of changing the way you target the first appointment is worth the reward of delivering better second and subsequent appointments.

No, I certainly can't *force* you to change the way you start the relationship with your prospect. I can only share my own experiences. Here are two.

A TRUE STORY ABOUT EFFECTIVE TARGETING ON THE FIRST APPOINTMENT

Not very long ago, one of the largest telecommunications hardware companies in the world wanted to see if their traditional $300,000-plus hardware sales could be conducted by inside salespeople—folks who sold exclusively by means of telephone, faxes, and e-mails and never met with their customers face to face.

It's important to note here that, before the VP of marketing launched this (cost-containing) brainstorm, this organization had never used its inside team to sell. These team members were "appointment setters" for the outside team, pure and simple. This selling model, by the way, was a popular one for many years; outside salespeople traditionally hated the task of appointment setting, and somehow they convinced the entire organization's top brass that this task was below them and should be done by someone else.

When Rich, the VP of marketing, called me, he complained that the company's cost of sales was totally out of control. He also felt that sales cycles were too long and that the company's existing customer market share was being pounded by the competition.

Rich had a big question for me: "Tony," he asked, "do you think it's possible to make a 300K sale over the telephone?"

My two-word answer—"Why not?"—was the fuel that sparked his dream.

We arranged for me to train his inside team. After we signed our agreement, I rolled up my sleeves and developed a process that resulted in 14 of 100 target chief information officers' (CIOs) booking a telephone appointment with one of the inside team members. All that was needed to justify my process was the first sale, which materialized in just 35 days. Bottom line: $286,000 in hardware sold by a salesperson that never left his cubicle.

ANOTHER TRUE STORY ABOUT EFFECTIVE
TARGETING ON THE FIRST APPOINTMENT

One of the largest employers in America is the U.S. Postal Service. Its most recent headcount in the sales department is 650.

These are noncommissioned salespeople. The VP of sales had a vision. He saw his entire team conducting a territory blitz on more than 6,000-targeted C-level corporate officers.

The VP of sales had a big question for me: "Tony," he said, "do you think it's possible to get a C-level officer to commit to an appointment with a representative of the U.S. Postal Service?"

My two-word answer—"Why not?"—sparked another dream.

The VP of sales and I agreed for me to train his people. After we signed our agreement, I rolled up my sleeves and developed a letter of introduction and a telephone dialogue that resulted in initial appointments representing more than $16 million in opportunities . . . in just one day's time.

Are you catching my drift here? Do you see what the 10th principle is?

10. *Aim for the top when you're setting the first appointment.*

Implementing the 10th principle or ignoring it is your choice.

Aim for the top on appointment number one, and you'll have a much better appointment number two, either with your high-level contact or with whomever he or she refers you to. That's my promise. If you follow all 10 principles outlined in this chapter, you'll have better first appointments, you'll have *more and better* second and subsequent appointments, and you'll be in a better position to make the sale in two calls.

GO BEYOND YOUR COMFORT ZONE

Putting the 10th principle into action is difficult for the average salesperson because the average salesperson is terrified of change. But I believe you're *not* the average salesperson, because the average salesperson wouldn't have made it this far in the book.

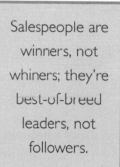

Salespeople are winners, not whiners; they're best-of-breed leaders, not followers.

Go beyond your comfort zone. Stretch yourself. Try what I'm suggesting. Make a commitment to at least attempt to implement the 10th principle for a week once you've completed this book—even if the first few interactions feel uncomfortable, even if it feels a little scary, even if this is not the way you're used to selling, even if this is not what you were trained to do by your sales manager, even if you're not crazy about the idea of changing your current routine because it seems to be working okay.

Salespeople who fail to make changes in their routine eventually lose. Salespeople who adapt to new realities, who try new things, and who implement better strategies eventually emerge as winners.

If you're a winner, please turn to Chapter 11.

FROM COACH STEVE

CRITICAL SALES SUCCESS STEPS—STEP 1: BUILD SALES
INSIDE LIFE INSTEAD OF LIFE INSIDE SALES

Between here and the end of the book, I will help you take a broader look at your sales career by guiding you through six Critical Sales Success Steps. This will be a parallel process along with Tony's guidance helping you master a new view of your selling routine. It will also enable you to more effectively integrate all of Tony's great ideas with the big picture view of your sales career. If you diligently follow my suggestions, while purposefully taking on Tony's challenges, you will finish this book with not only new skills, but also a master plan for success.

The first of the six Critical Sales Success Steps is to picture your successful sales career as one of many components in overall success in life. Many salespeople make the mistake of attempting to fit everything in life into their sales career. All their goals in life are connected to earning money in sales. Their decisions about how they spend their time always yield to "priorities" they have set for sales efforts. Family, recreation, fitness—everything comes after their focus on sales success. Thinking that a 100 percent commitment to sales success is the only pathway to peak performance, everything comes in behind their sales career in the order of priorities.

You want the truth? If the only top priority you have in life is sales, you will be unrelatable, unbalanced, and boring.

Think for a minute. What "lights you up"? At the end of your days on earth, what will you look back on as most gratifying or most fulfilling? Who will you want to have spent the most time with? What will give you the most pride or pleasure? My guess is that you won't say, "I mastered the 100-hour workweek."

If you truly want to be a success in sales, make *your sales career part of your life*—not *life part of your sales career.* Your success in sales will be directly related to your ability to relate to people, how well you maintain a high level of energy and enthusiasm, and your ability to walk away from the parts of the sales game that don't pay off in the context of what is really important in life. You can achieve these things only by having a broad, fulfilling array of goals and pursuits that you can relate to and engage in. Likewise, success in other areas of life will translate to a greater understanding of success in the sales career component of life.

Take the time before you move into the next chapter to start some notes in a special notebook or a separate section of the notes you are taking on Tony's ideas. Write down a description of what you want to be proud of in life from a broad perspective. Paint a mental picture (see Chapter 6 on the importance of visualization) of what you want *all* of life to look like. Sure, there will be tremendous sales success, but what else? What about family, friends, overall financial success, community, spiritual fulfillment, recreation—put it all in there. Don't worry about form or who is going to read it. This is just for you. Capture the big picture of life so that you have a context—a framework—within which to build ultimate success.

Just a reminder: If you have access to the Internet, go to www .gettingthesecondappointment.com and download the forms that are waiting for you to make this step and the ones to follow easier to create. You'll find them all in Tony's Success Portal.

11

THREE STRATEGIES
TO APPOINTMENT
SUCCESS

There is a Latin saying: *Finis Originae Pendit.* It means "The end depends upon the beginning." And that's certainly an important thought to keep in mind in any discussion of the second sales appointment.

Your chances of getting a productive second appointment (or, even better, closing the sale within two visits) are, of course, tied directly to the results of your first appointment. The results you get on your first appointment are, in turn, tied directly to three important preparatory steps. I call these the three keys to a successful first appointment. They are:

1. *Establishing* your target and building credibility before your first appointment.
2. *Knowing how to build rapport* with your prospect before the first appointment.
3. *Determining* (ahead of time) your contact's criteria for evaluating your message.

Let's look at each of these keys.

KEY #1: ESTABLISHING YOUR TARGET
AND BUILDING CREDIBILITY BEFORE
YOUR FIRST APPOINTMENT

In this part of the book, the word *prospect* means any enterprise in your sales territory that is a perfect fit to your TIP. (If you flipped to this chapter at random, and don't know what a TIP is, please start reading the book from the beginning!)

You must pick and qualify your prospects very carefully. By my estimate, more than 60 percent of the sales activity that we salespeople typically embark upon is done with the wrong prospects. This is a waste of time.

The simple fact that a person calls you doesn't make him or her a qualified prospect. The fact that a company is in your territory and within the industries that you typically sell to doesn't automatically mean that company is a qualified prospect. *You must highlight the best opportunities first!* Asking effective qualifying questions is an important part of this process.

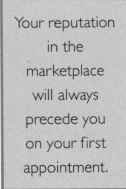

Your reputation in the marketplace will always precede you on your first appointment.

Early on in my sales career, I discovered the real importance of asking the right questions of the right person. After a two-year long sales cycle with a firm I'll call Acme, I was finally at the contract signing stage. I'd blown off the competition early on. The balance of this long, protracted sales cycle was consumed by initial evaluations, reliability tests, product studies, factory tours, on-site visits, evaluations of our evaluations, and the like. The voluminous RFP (Request For Proposal) and RFQ (Request For Quotation) I'd been working with made the *New World Encyclopedia* look like a quick-read paperback.

I had recruited the assistance of my company's presales support team and factory personnel to answer the pages and pages of Acme's questions. I didn't really have the time to do it all myself. As a matter of fact, I didn't really get a chance to *read* all of the responses we came up with. After all, I was the salesperson. I had better things to do!

Finally, the day we were all waiting for rolled around: the contract signing. I invited my sales manager to attend, and she invited our area manager to drop in. These are glory moments, after all, and you want everyone of consequence to be on hand. The general manager of the entire division of Acme had his pen in hand; at his side was his senior contracts administrator. As the pages flipped by, visions of plenty ran through my head of the commission checks to come, and all the toys they would bring. My dreams dissolved when I heard the general manager speak those terrifying words that every salesperson who has reached this phase of the sale dreads: "There's a problem here."

It seems that both I and my presales contracts support person had overlooked Acme's requirement of having five years of spare parts support. Our standard offering was three years. After a few whispers between the general manager and his contracts guy, the general manager said: "I'm sorry, but I can't sign this agreement until you modify your spare parts policy to five years."

My manager, her boss, and I walked out to my company car in total silence. As soon as we closed the doors, they both spoke the same sentence at the same time: "I thought you said we were going to get this deal!"

> Knowing when to say "no" is a trait that successful salespeople must master.

I reassured them both. After all, all we had to do was get the division to change a three to a five. How hard could that be?

But events back at the office later proved that what I wanted was not going to be easy to get. The division responsible for making the spare parts would not change the standard policy. So I booked an appointment with our CEO. That's right, the CEO of our entire organization. I figured that once *he* saw the magnitude of this opportunity, surely he would make the necessary decision and help us nail this sale.

Strike three! Despite what I felt was an airtight case for making this exception—a case that appealed to the revenue potential, the size of this customer, the add-on business, the brand recognition, the fact that we would have our first strong foothold in this part of the industry—my CEO responded with a memorable one-word answer: "No."

Then, out of sheer desperation, I restated my case. This time, the CEO gave considerable thought to his answer (by which I mean maybe three seconds) and then actually said: "Tony, what part of No don't you understand?"

If I had identified and paid close attention to the real *deal-breakers* in that account, I would have been able to walk away without investing two years of hard labor. Make no mistake—that would have been a real victory. I would have been free to pursue other more suitable, more promising, more profitable sales. If I'd asked Acme better questions, I would have been able to identify the *No* early on . . . and figure out that I actually had *No* sale.

Here then, are some questions you should consider asking to avoid making the mistake I made. Use these questions to *push for the no* during your first appointment. It's better to get it then rather than to waste time. As you consider the following questions, bear in mind the following selling rule:

The salesperson who loses early wins more often.

Ask the Recommender:

"What is the biggest problem you're having with regards to[X] in your department/team/operation?" (You should fill in this blank with the area of expertise reflected in your organization and its product, service, or solution.)

Listen carefully. When the answer you hear lines up with something your product, service and/or solution has the realistic possibility of delivering, you should immediately ask:

"What's your opinion? Would having a [X] (fill-in the blank with a function of your product, service, and/or solution) make your [job/task/responsibility] easier, faster, or more enjoyable?"

Ask the Influencer:

"What improvement(s) would you make to your current [X]?" (Here, again, fill in this blank with the precise area of expertise reflected in your organization and its product, service, or solution.)

Listen carefully. When the answer you hear lines up with the features of your product, service, and/or solution, you should immediately ask:

"In the past, what steps have you taken to create that type of change in your operations?"

Ask the Decision Maker:

"Are you currently looking for new ideas and improvement in any of the following three areas: [X]?" (Here you should fill in this blank with three areas where your product, service, or solution is likely to be of interest to the Decision Maker.)

Listen carefully. When the answer you hear lines up with something your organization has the capability to deliver, you should immediately ask:

"What must my organization do to prove to you that we can help you overachieve your [goal identified by Decision Maker] and earn the right to become one of your trusted business partners between now and the end of this [week, month, quarter, year]?"

Ask the Approver:

"What are your top three goals, plans, and objectives with regards to [X] for the next [month, quarter, year]?" (You should fill this blank with an area of expertise, benefit, or advantage associated your product, service, or solution.)

Listen carefully. When what you hear lines up with what your product, service, and/or solution has the capability of doing, then you should immediately ask:

If we can prove to you that we can exceed your expectations and help you overachieve your [Approver's goal/plan/objective] could you see yourself making an investment of [X] and becoming one of our customers between now and the end of this [week, month, quarter, year]?

I'm advocating that you attempt to make contact with Approvers early on in the process. To build credibility with them, ask the qualifying questions I've outlined here, and then follow my interviewing advice and the advice on broadcasting hard-dollar and soft-dollar value. (Both of these topics are covered in Chapter 5.)

When you get a No answer to your qualifying question from an Approver, you should walk away from the opportunity.

You read right—you should walk!

Over the past 10 years, I've been conducting mentoring sessions for the alumni of my seminars and the readers of my books. At first, we included tear-sheets that my student's could mail-in, then we graduated to using teleconferencing. Now I conduct my mentoring on a weekly basis using the Internet. Although the way I coach and mentor has changed over the years, many of the questions have stayed the same.

> People will always be busy; . . . however, people will always make time for those who can make their jobs a little easier and more rewarding.

Here's the most popular question; I've been dealing with it for a decade now: "What do you suggest I do when an Approver says they have no needs I can fulfill and no interest in working with my organization?"

And here's the answer to the question: "Walk away!"

Now, just about every time I give that answer, the salesperson says something pretty darn close to the following: "Don't you think I should call someone else in the organization and see if they have a need?"

Here's the one word answer: "No!"

You know the Approver doesn't want to work with you. Why put time into *anything* that will not yield the desired result of a sale and a commission? Be honest with yourself. Cut your losses and move on.

KEY #2: KNOW HOW TO BUILD RAPPORT WITH YOUR PROSPECT

The way you interact with your prospect before the first appointment will either demonstrate that you have the ability to build and maintain effective business rapport and equal business stature—or demonstrate that you don't have this ability.

If the latter is true, you *will not* get the first appointment (or, for that matter, the second appointment—or, for that matter, the sale).

There's a reliable principle you can take advantage of on this score. Simply put, *the sooner your contact gets back in touch with you, the greater the level of Business Rapport and Equal Business Stature you have established.* In other words, the sooner you hear from the person, the more of an equal you are.

Business Rapport simply means that you're ready, willing, and able to play on the same business level as the person sitting across the table from you. This applies to individuals you talk to over the telephone, leave voice mails for, or send written or electronic correspondence to. Business Rapport also means that you understand the other person's personality style and respect it.

Personality Styles

Salespeople typically ignore the personality styles of their prospects—and, by doing so, unintentionally offend those prospects.

Ignoring your prospect's personality style is a fatal error. It's one of those unfortunate situations where not knowing what you don't know really can sabotage your sales efforts. Once you make even an innocent mistake in this vitally important area, the odds are that you'll never get invited back again—without ever knowing the reason for your exile.

This is an area worth learning about. Here's the scoop: There are four distinctly different personality styles; each of us has a primary and a secondary style. Dr. David Merrill made this initial discovery in the late 1960s; he studied salespeople to develop what has become a cornerstone assessment in psychological studies. According to Dr. David, you (and I and every other human on planet earth) can be assigned to one of the following categories:

- *The Analytical Style:* These people tend to keep their emotions inside and mostly ask questions when in conversations with others. (These folks may be perceived as introverted.)
- *The Expressive Style:* These individuals tend to show their emotions freely and openly, and their conversation has

more of a telling style. (These folks may be perceived as outgoing.)

- *The Amiable Style:* These folks tend to easily show and share their emotions, but are similar to the Analytic Style in that their conversational style is essentially one of asking. (These folks may be perceived as nurturing.)
- *The Driver Style:* Similar to the Analytic Style, they tend to keep their true emotions inside, but their conversation is more of a telling nature, which is similar to the Expressive Style. (These folks may be perceived as aggressive.)

I know this seems a bit simplistic but, when you get right down to it, we humans are pretty easy to read—if you know what to look for.

It's extremely important to know your own style and the style of your prospect. Why? Certain style pairs get along very well together—and others don't. I am not suggesting that you'll be changing your primary style (that's not possible). What I am going to suggest, however, is that you determine your prospect's style and then respect it.

• • •

Let's determine what your style is. On Figure 11.1 that follows, put an X on the spot that corresponds to your answers to the following two questions. *Hint:* Stay away from answers like "it

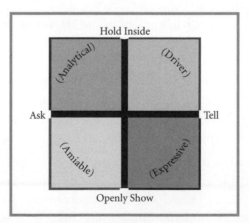

FIGURE 11.1 Style chart.

depends on the situation . . ." or, "only when someone else. . . ." Just stick with your initial response and put an X on the chart. There is no right or wrong answer here.

1. Place an X on the line that leads to "Hold Inside" if it's hard for others to tell when you're excited or how you feel about a certain issue. The more you hold your emotions inside the closer your X should be to the words "Hold Inside." If you use a great deal of body language when you communicate and your facial expressions are highly animated and you openly show your emotions, place an X close to the line that leads to the words: "Openly Show."

2. If your conversational style tends toward the controlling (if not dominating) side, place an X close to the line that leads to "Tell." The greater you tendency to control a conversation, the closer your X should be placed toward "Tell." (Note that it's possible to control a conversation without being talkative.) If you can't remember the last time you interrupted someone, or rarely interrupt other people, you should place an X close to the line that leads to "Ask."

Now, connect your Xs by drawing horizontal and vertical lines until they intersect, and you have defined your personality style.

Now, that you know what your style is, you're going to find out how to determine your prospect's style. Take a look at the following characteristics and think of your last discussion with a specific prospect. Which set of categories comes closest to describing him or her?

Analytic Style
The Analytic Style is usually shown by those in the following positions: programmer, engineer, scientist, CPA/accountant, project leader, planner.

Key Attributes
- Loves details, facts, figures, charts, spreadsheets.
- Deliberate in their actions.
- Solitary, prefers process over interaction with others.

- Accuracy and timeliness are hallmarks.
- Low tolerance for mistakes or misinformation.
- Critical but dislikes receiving criticism.
- Does things "by the book" and will not break the rules.
- Ultimate problem solvers.

Expressive Style

The person with an Expressive Style tends to hold positions in marketing, sales, public relations, and communications.

Key Attributes

- Loves dealing with people and teams.
- Volunteers to be in the center of enjoyable and challenging new activities.
- Loves change.
- Loves attention.
- Not strong on follow-up.
- Excellent motivators.
- Excellent barnstormers.

Amiable Style

The person with an Amiable Style tends to hold positions in customer service, support, administrative positions, human resources, and counselors.

Key Attributes

- Great listeners.
- Nurturers.
- Helpful.
- Don't like the limelight.
- Relationships are critically important.
- Don't like high-pressure situations.
- Won't choose sides.
- Indecisive.

Driver Style

You'll find the Driver Style individual in positions like captain of the ship, an entrepreneur, president, CEO, vice president, plant manager, or any position that has the hint of leader associated with it.

Key Attributes

- Big egos.
- Brief, direct, and to the point.
- Big on authority.
- Must be in the "know."
- Likes to delegate.
- Decisive.
- Competitive.
- Driven.
- Tough-skinned.
- Likes to write and break the rules.

> Knowing your style is just as important as knowing your prospect's style.

Interacting with Different Personality Styles

Can you see the style of your last prospect among the four we just detailed? I thought so.

Keep the following principles in mind whenever you're in an appointment with a prospect. I can guarantee that if you ignore what follows you'll have little or no chance of getting a second appointment. (Refer back to the styles chart on page 120 as necessary.)

1. People with the same styles do not necessarily get along or work well together.
2. Styles that are situated on the chart directly across from or perpendicular to each other generally have a more difficult time working together.
3. Styles that are situated on the chart that are "up and down" from each other are more likely to interact harmoniously.

Being sensitive to the other person's communication style means, for instance, that you:

- Don't force an Analytic to break the rules or skip a step.
- Don't ask an Expressive to follow up on details or perform a mundane analysis.
- Don't expect an Amiable to take sides or speak up and make a decision.

- Never try to get Drivers to engage in conversations in which they do not feel like they have the upper hand.

Respect the other person's behavior; don't try to change it. If you do this, you'll be in a much stronger position to win the second appointment.

The fastest way to build effective Business Rapport is to have Equal Business Stature. Having Equal Business Stature means that:

- You are the functional equivalent of the person you're working with in your prospect's organization—regardless of whether that person's title puts him or her in the boiler room to the boardroom.
- You have or can attain an equal understanding of some (but not all) of this person's current business problems.
- You have ideas about how to solve some of these problems.
- You have the ability to articulate your idea(s) in a way that this person can easily understand.
- You have the ability (and the right!) to change the other person's thinking by presenting your idea(s).

The Building Blocks of Business Rapport and Equal Business Stature

> If "title to title" were really the rule by which the business world operated, no one would sell much of anything.

Here are some ideas on building business rapport and equal business stature. First and foremost, remember that it's not a good idea to allow external factors like your prospect's title, social stature, appearance, or current situation to do your thinking for you. In other words, don't let the fact that your prospect's title happens to be Head Scientist, Chief Financial Officer, or Chief Executive Officer intimidate you. Remind yourself constantly that you have the right to communicate with *anyone* in the organization.

Second, follow these simple guidelines while interacting with your prospect:

- Make sure your passion and enthusiasm matches or is slightly higher than that of your prospect.
- Be constantly upbeat and optimistic, such that you support your prospects' best view of themselves, their company, and their current situation.
- Stay focused on the scope of your prospect's picture. In other words, if your contact is tightly focused, you should be, too. If your contact takes a "wide-angle" view of the world, so should you.
- Propose ideas that *directly* address your prospect's current situation. Remember, you're setting up a first appointment. Far-in-the future payoffs and "pie-in-the-sky" ideas will be better received at a later time.
- Be persuasive. Note that *persuasive* is not synonymous with *deceptive* or *controlling*. Your underlying message must always be a simple one: "I have a strong belief in what I am saying, and that's why I want you to believe in me." Mean it!
- Make sure that you've got a sound grip on the hard and soft dollar value you can realistically expect to deliver. (See Chapter 20.) If you try to fake it, you'll face an uphill battle when it comes to building Business Rapport and Equal Business Stature.
- Articulate your idea(s) to solve this prospect's problems in a way that he or she can easily understand.

KEY #3: DETERMINING YOUR CONTACT'S CRITERIA FOR EVALUATING YOUR MESSAGE

We've already decided that we have four categories of individuals we will interact with: Recommender, Influencer, Decision Maker, and Approver. (And you also know by now which one of these people you should target as a first contact.)

The question is—what represents a "win" for each of these individuals? What are their personal criteria for the relationship likely to be?

To understand their personal criteria, it helps to understand the person. This is where the work of the psychologist Abraham Maslow comes in handy.

Once you understand what's commonly referred to as *Maslow's pyramid* and learn how to put it to good use, you'll peg your prospect's personal definition of a "win." (You'll also find it much easier to build Business Rapport and Equal Business Stature.)

Maslow's pyramid is an ascending five-stage grouping of human needs. Its basic principle is that humans (you, me, your prospect, Bill Gates, the president, and everybody else you can think of) must be satisfied from the bottom (or base) of the pyramid upward. In other words, we don't focus on any need until we've satisfied the first, or foundation-level need, then we work our way up.

As you can see in Figure 11.2, Maslow placed physiological needs related to a supportive physical environment (sleep, shelter, food, and water) at the base of the pyramid. Next came "safety and security," or the need to protect loved ones, possessions, and us. Next came "belonging and recognition" needs, those related to personal,

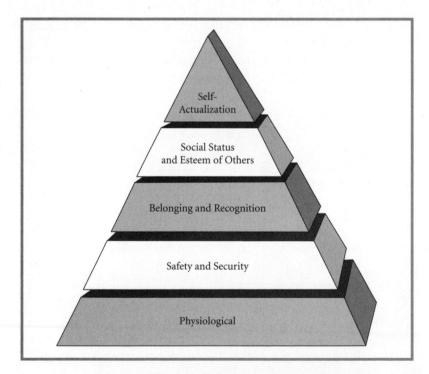

FIGURE 11.2   Maslow's hierarchy of needs.

family, and professional accomplishments and the recognition of them. Second from the top came "social status, self-respect, and esteem granted from others," a category that reflects needs related to a sense of ranking within social systems. At the top of the heap is "self-actualization," or the need associated with experiencing life to the fullest. (This need can be expressed in any number of different ways depending on the individual.)

Based on my experience over the years, I've kept track of what I've found to be typical wins for each of the four categories in the corporate hierarchy—broken down within Maslow's hierarchy of needs:

Physiological (Base of the Pyramid):

- *Maslow objectives:* Supportive physical environment; sleep, shelter, food, and water.
- *Parallel issues in the corporate world:* Mergers, acquisitions, downsizing, re-deploying of employees, labor issues, hiring, firing, performance reviews, equipment, and process that impact individual's work, environment, and workplace ergonomics, efficiencies, and effectiveness.

Physiological Concerns as Applied to:

- *Recommender:* Getting hired, getting fired, workplace ergonomics, easier processes to work with.
- *Influencer:* Getting hired, getting fired, equipment and processes, workflow, performance, form-fit-function evaluations.
- *Decision Maker:* Getting hired, getting fired, re-deploying of resources and team members, downsizing, re-engineering, performance reviews.
- *Approver:* Survival of the organization, labor issues, mergers, acquisitions, and fiscal responsibilities.

If an Approver is deeply engaged in a merger, it's doubtful that he or she will be interested in meeting with a salesperson about anything other than how that person could assist in making the merging activity work to everyone's best advantage. Therefore, if your aim is to get an approval on replacing a piece of equipment or service that happens to be working right now except for a few new whiz-bang features that the Influencer is all jazzed about, don't hold your breath in the hope of winning the Approver to your cause.

Safety and Security:

- *Maslow objectives:* Protection of our loved ones, our possessions, and ourselves.
- *Parallel issues in the corporate world:* Protection of customer base, economic fluctuation, stock valuation, and security against competitive assaults, holding on to key employees.

Safety and Security Concerns as Applied to:

- *Recommender:* Job security.
- *Influencer:* Turf and domain/department security, hoarding of responsibilities.
- *Decision Maker:* Keeping key employees, promotions to higher levels of influence and authority.
- *Approver:* Stock valuations, economic conditions, and the impact they have on top-, middle-, and bottom-line performance.

It really doesn't take much to trigger someone's need for safety and security. Recently, the Approver of one of my largest customers decided to close all sales offices and have all the members of the sales team work from their homes. This was a big win for the Approver. She was able to lower expenses and show a large boost in earnings on the heels of a very big merger. However, this created a big, big problem for many of the sales team. Already jolted by the merger, changes in territories, commission, and compensation plans, they felt as though they were being left out, that the change in locale meant the beginning of the end for them at that company. They felt tremendously insecure. As a result, many of them bailed out and found new jobs with major competitors who had a more traditional infrastructure of support and interaction. *Lesson:* What appears as a win for one is not always a win for all.

Social Status:

- *Maslow objectives:* Self-respect, esteem from others, a sense of value and rank within a social system.
- *Parallel issues in the corporate world:* Leadership, creating followers, recognition, accomplishing vision and mission statements, winning the respect of team members, employee loyalty, empire-building, protecting turf, respecting chains of command.

Social Status Concerns as Applied to:

- *Recommender:* Winning perks, career advancement, receiving awards and trophies, being nominated for the "team player of the month/quarter/year" award, being thanked, being praised publicly, getting a high five, being motivated with a carrot rather than a stick.
- *Influencer:* Being in control, career advancement, building a bigger personal "empire" within the organization, having a say in what's going on and taking place, making sure that both insiders and outsiders play by the rules.
- *Decision Maker:* Being seen as a leader/advisor/mentor, career advancement, having the respect of peers and team members, winning higher internal or external visibility.
- *Approver:* Over-accomplishing the mission.

If you sell outsourcing human resources services, then you basically replace human resources departments. Sometimes you retain employees, sometimes you don't; in either case, you cut costs. In the latter, you cut jobs. Let's say you're calling on an Influencer and describing your product, service, and solution capabilities and how they align with their department's needs. At the conclusion of the meeting you ask, "Who besides yourself will be involved in making this decision?" Watch what happens. The answer is always "nobody." You have (unintentionally) shown this Influencer that you are challenging him or her in terms of value and rank; you have run into an Influencer whose empire building is more important than over-achieving corporate strategic initiatives. You're challenging this person's social status concerns. And, as a result, you're going nowhere with this sale.

Self-Actualization:

- *Maslow objectives:* The experience of reaching one's full potential and experiencing life to the fullest.
- *Parallel issues in the corporate world:* Professional challenges, expanding horizons, winning stock options, winning invitations to board seats or other prestigious positions, getting a raise/bonus/promotion, professional and personal growth opportunities.

Self-Actualization Concerns as Applied to:

- *Recommender:* Learning something new, getting a new task/responsibility, expanding career opportunities, expanding personal skills development as a result of new job responsibilities.
- *Influencer:* Expanding empires and responsibilities, gaining additional power over key organizational decisions, professional/intellectual growth, being on the cutting edge (preferably without noticeable risk).
- *Decision Maker:* An invitation to sit on the board of directors or advisors.
- *Approver:* Achieving a long-term business goal, getting the "golden parachute," taking advantage of a robust exit strategy, being seen as the "leader of the year," getting on the cover or front page of trade/business journals for ethical accomplishments, pursuing noteworthy philanthropic endeavors.

Not long ago, I approached one of the world's most prominent executives, asking him to write the foreword to one of my books. Based on my discussion with his enthusiastic executive assistant, I felt sure he'd accept. A few weeks later, though I got word that he had declined the opportunity . . . not because he didn't like the book, but because he was preparing for a long-distance hot-air balloon adventure! For him, that journey was a personal challenge more important than the recognition or visibility he might enjoy as the result of participating in any best-selling book project. He was focused on self-actualization.

MATCHING THE CRITERIA

Except for those unfortunate individuals who are manic or clinically depressed, we all want to win. It's just a question of defining what constitutes *a win*—and how we as salespeople identify those win criteria and help people meet them.

If you want to create winning relationships with anyone in the organization (Recommender, Influencer, Decision Maker, and/or Approver), you must understand how each of your products, services, and solutions can apply to each level of Maslow's pyramid for each category of individual.

Prepare ahead of time. Take a good, long look at the summary that appears above and then ask yourself how it applies to *your* target prospect at a given organization. On a separate sheet of paper, write down specific ideas about how you can position your products, services, and solutions *before* the face-to-face meeting to appeal to this person in each of the five areas we've discussed. Then be open to clues that will show you where on the pyramid your contact is operating and which need you should be focusing on:

- *Physiological:* Do you have any ideas that will help the business survive? How can you create a more stable, enjoyable, reliable working environment for your prospect?
- *Safety and security:* What ideas do you have to address each of your prospect's need for an overall feeling of safety and security?
- *Belonging and recognition:* What can your products, services, and solutions do to help win or create a value-added situation for the individual or department? Do you have any ideas that can turn an expense into a profit—and thereby win positive recognition for your prospect?

> If your ideas match the Maslow need level of your prospect, you will make the sale.

- *Social status:* How can your products, services, and solutions enhance the perceived status of the organization or the individual?
- *Self-actualization:* Does this person/department/ organization seem to be already at the top of their mountain of accomplishments? If so, be ready to ask questions like, "What would happen if . . . ?" and "What are the three most disappointing results you've experienced in the last [six months]?" Lay down a challenge. (That's what people in self-actualization mode are hungriest for.)

One of the best ways to win the second appointment—and, eventually, to make the sale—is to try to determine, during your premeeting contacts, where the individual you're calling on is likely to be situated on Maslow's pyramid. In other words, try to narrow down the possible Maslow criterion they'll be using to evaluate the meeting. Make it a game. Try to come up with your best guess about whether this person is operating from a physiological, safety and security, belonging and recognition, social status, or self-actualization position. With just a little practice, you'll be able to determine, almost instantly, the one or two most likely hierarchy-of-need candidates.

During your face-to-face meeting, you can then *confirm* your initial diagnosis—or alter it if it's wrong. Then, before the first meeting concludes, suggest a course of action that dramatically and directly addresses the person's *correct* Maslow need level.

Rest assured that, if you do this, you'll win the second appointment . . . and, in all likelihood, a long-term business ally.

LOCK IN WHAT YOU'VE LEARNED

I invite you to participate in an e-learning exercise that I've developed based on this chapter. Visit www.gettingthesecondappointment .com and then click on Chapter 11 Online Assets. You'll get a chance to take a personalities style assessment and download additional information.

12

YOUR
APPOINTMENT
AGENDAS

As you read this page, millions of salespeople are reaching out to millions of prospects. How many of these salespeople ask themselves the following question *before* picking up the telephone: *What, exactly, would I like to discuss during my first discussion/ appointment with a new prospect?*

How would *you* answer that question, given the following options?

A: Mostly product-related topics.

B: Mostly business-related topics.

C: Both A and B.

Please answer the question before you proceed with this chapter.

• • •

If you picked C, you failed! You're trying to have it both ways.

If you picked A, you didn't do much better. You probably fall within the 70 percent of salespeople who are typically behind quota, because they spend too much (or all) of their time with Recommenders and Influencers.

If you picked B, odds are you are or soon will be *ahead* of quota. You know that the main reason to have a first appointment is to learn about the priorities of Decision Makers and Approvers—to find out about *their* business priorities and determine what kind of potential relationship *they* may envision with you. Specifics about the products and services you offer come later and may involve other people in the organization.

> It's doubtful that you'll find one prospect who will want to talk about both technical and business issues.

Let me go a little bit further with this point. There is really no way you can expect to find one individual in the target organization who will be able to discuss both technical and business topics to a level of proficiency that will satisfy your sales process. Think of Italian salad dressing: Its basic ingredients are oil and vinegar. You can shake it all you want, but when you let it sit for any length of time, you're back to oil and vinegar.

In organizations all across America, technical people talk about technical stuff, and business-oriented people talk about business stuff. The right hand often doesn't really know (or care) what the left hand is doing. When asked about "business initiatives," technical types say things like, "Those kinds of details are left to the 'higher-ups'; we don't need to concern ourselves with the budget. We'll get whatever it takes." When forced into topics of a technical nature, senior executives say things like: "I have people on my staff that look into these types of issues, hold-on, let me connect you."

News flash: We need to speak the language of the person we're talking to during the first appointment. (And every other appointment.)

Has it ever happened to you that as you discussed the functions and features of your product/service/solution, the Recommender and/or Influencer you were talking to was sitting at the edge of his or her chair leaning forward into your topic but when you moved into the topic of advantages and benefits, your contact began to fidget around uncomfortably? Has that same person promised to follow up with you after the meeting . . . and never did so?

Now you know why that sort of thing happens: *You were speaking the wrong language and using the wrong agenda.*

Once you complete this chapter, you'll have no excuse for making that mistake ever again.

It's best to keep a particular prospect in mind when you create your agenda for the first meeting. In shaping your agenda for the first meeting, you want everything you do and every issue you raise to be tailored to the individual's need and their perspective.

Before you build your agenda around the time-tested formula of Functions, Features, Benefits, and Advantages, look more closely at these elements and decide which ones you really want to spend your time evaluating.

FUNCTIONS

Pick up any owner's manual, operator's manual, or policy and you'll be as close to the bone to Functions as you'll ever want to be. Basically, Functions are all about *how* to use whatever it is that you sell.

Take a moment and list four Functions related to your products, services, and solutions. Write them down on a separate sheet of paper before you continue with this chapter.

• • •

FEATURES

Pick up the hood of any car (my personal favorite is a Corvette) and take a look. You'll see the pieces, components, and parts that make up the engine. Now, put that car up on a lift and examine the undercarriage: You'll see the springs, shocks, transmission, and so on.

You've been looking at features. These are the specific parts and components that make up the whole of whatever it is you happen to be selling (or looking at).

Take a moment and list four Features of your products, services, and solutions. Write them down on a separate sheet of paper before continuing in this chapter.

• • •

Functions are how you use what it is you're selling.

Features are the parts that make up what it is you're selling.

Advantages explain the many ways your product gives your prospect an edge.

ADVANTAGES

How do you provide an edge with your products, services, and solutions? What is the value you *personally* provide to your prospects and customers? For instance, in what ways do you provide ideas, advice, brainstorming, and consulting during your sales process to tailor what you deliver to your customers?

If, during your sales process, you help solve problems that are independent of what it is you happen to be selling, you have an advantage over your competition, and your prospects will clearly see the advantages of doing business with you.

Advantages add a dimension to your products, services, and solutions that no Function or Feature can.

Take a moment and think of four Advantages of your products, services, and solutions. Write them down on a separate sheet of paper before you proceed.

• • •

BENEFITS

Benefits can be defined in three words: Results, results, results! How does your product, service, solutions, and value-added offering positively affect your prospect's performance? How long will it take your prospect/customer to realize such results? What's the hard and/or soft dollar value that you can deliver or suspect that you can deliver?

Whenever you think in terms of sustained improvements in the areas of revenues, efficiencies, market share, shareholder value, fixed expenses, or variable expense, or any combination of those elements, you're thinking in terms of Benefits.

Take a moment and think of four Benefits your organization offers. Write them down on a separate sheet of paper before you continue with this chapter.

• • •

WHAT'S NEXT?

With a firm grip on the Functions, Features, Advantages, and Benefits of our products, services, and solutions let's divide them into two very different categories, so we can shape our first-appointment agenda intelligently.

Functions and Features—Technical Criteria

Technical Criteria have nothing to do with who you sell for, but everything to do with *what* you sell. This information is typically found on formal documentation that explains everything about your product. This is the form, fit, and function of what you sell.

If you sell life insurance, this category embraces the terms and conditions of the policy. If you sell forklifts, it's the capacities and specifications that are in the operator's manual or shop manual. If you sell pharmaceuticals, this category reflects the ingredients and prescriptions of the medications that you represent.

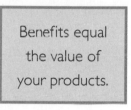

Benefits equal the value of your products.

Recommenders and Influencers are best suited to discuss *technical criteria*. If you've scheduled your first appointment with them (and I hope you haven't, but if you have), technical criteria is what you'll want to talk about.

Bottom line: Exploring and Initiating about technical criteria is best done with Recommenders and Influencers—not Decision Makers and Approvers.

FIRST-APPOINTMENT ISSUES FOR
THE RECOMMENDER

Remember, this is the player who will most likely *use* whatever it is that you happen to be selling. Focus on the reality of what's going on today . . . not what you have to offer in the future.

Consider asking:

- What would make it easier for you to [create presentations]?
- How do you currently [post a deposit] into your [accounting] system?
- What's been your experience with [getting defects repaired]?

- Who in your organization is held most responsible for [time-to-revenue] initiatives?
- What was happening before your department installed their new [inventory control] system?

Take a moment and write down four ideas for questions you might ask a Recommender on the first meeting, spun around Technical Criteria and Functions. (It's best to use the same sheet of paper you listed your functions on.)

· · ·

FIRST-APPOINTMENT ISSUES FOR THE INFLUENCER

These individuals have the power to change the minds of others. They are the all-important advisors to the Decision Makers.

For the most part, as we've seen, these folks (1) hate to be sold to and (2) hate people who try to sell to them. Strict adherence to technical criteria is in order. Assuming that you have, for some reason, scheduled a first appointment with an Influencer, your discussion should be built around questions like:

- What do you like most about your [hard-copy output devices]?
- What do you like least about your [direct mail strategies]?
- If you could redesign your [accounting system] what features would you include?
- Tell me about your [sales training] program.
- What [tolerance] do you want the [input/output] of your [power supply] to be?
- What do you think about [having a document retrieval] system that would allow for [immediate access with total security features]?

Take a moment and write down four ideas for questions you might ask an Influencer on the first meeting, relating to technical criteria and features. (It's best to use the same sheet of paper you listed your features on.)

• • •

Never, ever deviate from topics of technical criteria with Recommenders and Influencers. Stay away from statements/questions that may be perceived as challenging, or that imply that you want a decision to be made. This means avoiding questions like:

- What's your budget?
- Who else are you considering?
- Who besides yourself will be involved in this decision?
- How soon will you be making your decision?
- What can I do to earn your business?
- If you had to make your decision right now what would it be?

> Technical criteria is all about the products you sell. Business criteria is all about the company you sell for.

Any one of these questions will put you into the *selling* role and doing so will result in your prospect saying something along the lines of: "I can't tell you that." You'll catapult yourself into the "stall mode" indefinitely.

Advantages and Benefits—Business Criteria

In the final analysis, business criteria have no association at all with what you sell. These concerns are product-independent.

Business criteria have *everything* to do, however, with the organization you sell for. What's at issue are subjects like corporate culture, brand awareness, and reputation. Business criteria is what typically shows up in annual reports, company visions, and mission statements. Business criteria has to do with past, present, and future reputation and image in the market space. Business criteria is about answering the question: "Should we have a relationship with this organization?"

The answer to that question frequently takes into account such factors as company policies, practices, and procedures; visibility in the community; support for philanthropic causes; benefits policies; and such public-perception issues as advertising styles; and the image of the person at the top. I've seen more than one sale in my career that was lost on an organization's business criteria—even though the company completely dominated the competition in the areas of technical criteria, performance, and compliance.

A True Story

The account manager of a large telecommunications company had his customer—a global tobacco company—sewn up. They were loyal customers and the deal was won on the telecom dominance in the area of technical superiority in data transmission speed, accuracy, and dependability. The telecom firm's technical performance record was flawless: 99.97 percent up-time over the most recent 18 months.

But one day, the CEO of the telecom company decided to make an announcement that UPI picked up: From that day forward, all 3,700 internationally located offices and manufacturing facilities were declared smoke-free environments.

Well, looking out for the health of employees is certainly important. Who could disagree?

You've already guessed the answer, I'm sure. It took exactly two days for the word to come down from the top echelons of the global tobacco company—and for the director of Information Systems to call the telecom company's account rep and deliver the bad news: "We're switching back to our old carrier." The uptime statistics, the past history, the great service—none of it mattered. The relationship was over.

Never underestimate the power of business criteria!

FIRST-APPOINTMENT ISSUES FOR
THE DECISION MAKER AND THE APPROVER

First appointments with the Decision Maker and the Approver should focus on business criteria—on how they run *their* business or work group, and what kinds of benefits and advantages they're looking for.

The primary interest of Decision Makers and Approvers is *not* in your products, services, and solutions per se. Rather, they are interested in the relationships that can deliver results, value, and benefits.

Early in my sales career I sold computer systems for Hewlett Packard (HP). We were known as an engineering company at that time and my first few years were spent selling "number crunches" to the scientific community.

I did great business, because the scientific community put a premium on HP's superior brainpower and expertise. Then, HP took its superior technology and plunged into the exciting new field of making business computers. I liked the idea and took on a new territory, selling HP's new entry into the market of finance, manufacturing, and distribution computer solutions.

My major competitor was IBM, which was known as the "business machine" company. Now, our computers were faster, more reliable, and less expensive than IBM's. Yet IBM won time after time. It was a painful experience for me to go from kicking butt to getting my butt kicked! To this day, HP carries that stigma—reputation—of being an engineering company first and foremost. You see, an advantage is really in the eyes of the beholder.

First-Appointment Issues for Decision Makers

These all-important individuals have complete control of the who, what, when, where, why, how, and how much of the decisions that eventually get made. You'll recall their job is to say "yes."

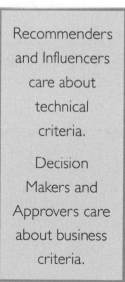

Recommenders and Influencers care about technical criteria.

Decision Makers and Approvers care about business criteria.

They control the masses, the troops, and the workforce and are held responsible for the timely completion and the over-achievement of the Approver's goals, plans, and objectives. Simply put: Decision Makers are important players. As we've seen, your sales career will take a quantum leap forward when you pro-actively recruit the Decision Maker as your sponsor.

When you're having a first appointment conversation with a Decision Maker, it's best to plant your feet firmly on the ground in areas that this individual is responsible for. This all-important player must quickly understand that there is the potential for value in a relationship with *you as an individual.* Once the Decision Maker has concluded this is the case, he or she will consider sponsoring you and your ideas.

Accordingly, you should ask questions like:

- What's the best way for my organization to support your needs with your [just-in-time supply chain management project]?

Important Note: The words "for my organization" (as opposed to "for my product") points us in the right direction and sets the all-important tone of a business-to-business relationship that can bring value. We are *not* interested in exploring product-to-business ideas with this person.

- What resources do you need in your [transportation] division to achieve your goals of [expansion into the Canadian marketplace] between [now and the end of this year]?
- If you had to pick your [business partner], [provider], [supplier] of choice right now who would it be?
- Who are the individuals that you hold most responsible for evaluating your [network] requirements?
- Who are the team players you look to for advice regarding [office equipment]?
- What elements made your last initiative in the area of [inventory control] a success?
- Would you be willing to advise me on the best ways to introduce my ideas to your [engineering] department?
- What are the top [three] areas of performance you look for in a [office equipment] provider?

Under *no* circumstances should you initiate a discussion of your product's features or functions with the Decision Maker. Even if these folks invite you to speak about your products, do so by describing benefits and advantages.

Take a moment and write down four questions you might raise with a Decision Maker during the first meeting, spun around business criteria and advantages. Don't continue reading this chapter until you've completed this assignment. (It's best to use the same sheet of paper you listed your advantages on.)

First-Appointment Issues with Approvers

These are movers and shakers. Approvers like to be at the wheel, with both feet on the accelerator. They are the ultimate "eyes-on-the-prize" individuals. For Approvers, obstacles are opportunities, problems are ways to exercise their creative powers, and sitting idle is the only unforgivable sin.

The Approver's role is of paramount importance to the outcome of your sale. The time you spend with these individuals must be well planned and purposeful. If you are going to "wing" any dialogue with anyone, make sure it's not with the Approver—the person who is in a position to spend the money and make the buy, who has no budget and who possesses the ultimate veto power.

Follow the Approver's lead, but be ready to provide specific details about the potential benefits of a business relationship with you and your organization. Ask questions like:

- [Sixty-five of the Fortune 100 companies] have taken our ideas and improved [time-to-market while at the same time lowering nonvalue expenses]. What's the best way for me to share our ideas with you and your organization between now and the end of this business day?
- What expectations do you personally have of an organization who can bring new ideas to the table about (benefit your organization has a track record of delivering) between now and the end of this [month, quarter, year]?
- If our organization can exceed your expectations, can you see any reason you would not want to become a business partner of ours between let's say now and the end of this fiscal [quarter]?

Looking for a quick sale of a new product? Call an Approver in your territory.

If you happen to be selling anything that has not been proven yet, is brand new, or has yet to be put to the test and you're struggling with proving its hard dollar value to your marketplace, my advice would be to schedule a face-to-face appointment with every single Approver in your territory. Why would you want to "admit" your lack of customers to someone at that level? Because Approvers are the only people in the organization who will understand and appreciate the trials and tribulations of taking a new product to market. Basically, what you want to say to the Approver in this situation is:

- We have a reasonable suspicion that we can deliver [benefit], and we're looking for an early adopter to prove that to be true. What we're offering could turn out to be an edge in your industry that only you would have. What's the best way for me to share our ideas with you and your organization?

You may be surprised at the speed and enthusiasm with which your Approver asks for more details.

Take a moment and write down four ideas for questions you might raise with an Approver during the first meeting, spun around business criteria. Don't keep reading this chapter until you've completed this assignment. (It's best to use the same sheet of paper you listed your benefits on.)

• • •

YOUR APPOINTMENT MATRIX

By now, you know what you're going to talk about and with whom you'll be talking on the first appointment. Figure 12.1 is what the

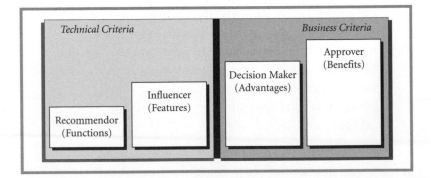

FIGURE 12.1   Appointment matrix.

matrix looks like; notice that your first appointment plan of attack is a summary of everything we've discussed so far in the book.

One last question . . . *where,* ideally, would you prefer to begin the relationship with the prospect company?

LOCK IN WHAT YOU'VE LEARNED

I invite you to participate in an e-learning exercise that I've developed based on this chapter. Visit www.gettingthesecondappointment .com and then click on Chapter 12 Online Assets. You'll get a chance to download an appointment matrix and other valuable information.

13

YOUR FOUR GOALS FOR THE FIRST MEETING

I n this chapter, we cover what you want to accomplish during your first appointment.

TELL 'EM, SELL 'EM

First, a word about what you *don't* want to accomplish. There's a chronic problem we salespeople have when it comes to dealing with prospects. We tend to "over-educate" them.

Why do we do this? Because we associate the process of education of our products, services, and solutions with selling. We figure the more a prospect knows, the quicker he or she will buy, and the *more* the prospect knows, the bigger the order will be.

Ready for the truth? Too much information too early in the sales process will cost you the sale. The more information prospects have early on, the less they need you. Too much information on the first appointment makes it harder to get the second appointment ("You've really given me a lot to think about . . .") and the harder it is to get the second appointment, the harder it is to make the sale.

WHAT *SHOULD* YOU TRY TO ACCOMPLISH
DURING THE FIRST APPOINTMENT?

What, then, are your goals? It's your first face-to-face meeting. On one end is a prospect with problems who knows little or nothing of how you can help solve them. On the other end is the salesperson—you—possessing a wealth of information, value, and mastery in selling skills. Right smack in the middle is the sale.

You've already established that your prospect fits your TIP. You've got a firm grip on the hard and soft value you can deliver, and you're poised with the tools to build business rapport and equal business stature.

By my estimate and experience, there are four different but complimentary goals on the first appointment:

1. Create your best first and last impression.
2. Establish yourself as an expert by confidently answering the question (spoken or unspoken): "What do you know about my industry?"
3. Present with conviction the ideas you have to improve on your prospect's current situation(s).
4. Create specific action item(s) for both you and your prospect with the common denominator of time.

> Over educating your prospect will kill your sale.

Items 2, 3, and 4 will, remarkably enough, follow naturally upon item 1, assuming you've followed all the advice that appears in the earlier chapters of this book. Item one actually takes a little bit of practice and insight to pull off convincingly, and so that's what we're going to spend our time on in this chapter.

ENTRANCES AND EXITS

The old adage "You only get one chance to make a first impression" is false. There are, by my count, *two* opportunities to make your first impression: One when you arrive and one when you depart.

This principle applies to everything we do: in-person meetings, telephone conversations, voice mail messages, e-mail messages, other written correspondence, and e-presentations.

Let's start with some thoughts on face-to-face meetings. Avoid at all cost using what's typically called an *ice-breaker*. Ice-breakers are for ships, not salespeople! You're familiar with how it's supposed to work, of course: Take the time to reduce tension by starting off with a reference to something you see in your prospect's office or lobby . . . or by making some trivial remark about something you happen to know about the other person.

This is a big mistake. Who's tense anyway? Certainly, not the prospect! The risk of using an ice-breaking statement is *huge*. Consider the following scenario:

> As the young salesperson walks into the prospect's office, he gives a quick glance at a picture on the vice president's credenza. In a quick and somewhat careless move to build rapport and reduce tension, the rep says: "Wow! How did you manage to get your picture taken with John Madden?"
>
> The prospect's answer ended the appointment. "That's not John Madden . . . that's my wife!"

I know this scenario sounds unbelievable. Trust me, though, it's true. If you doubt its validity, you can see it on www.salesautopsy.com.

Having made a commitment to avoid pointless chitchat, you will greet, shake hands, and exchange business cards with the prospect. When you accept your prospect's business card make sure that you follow this procedure:

> First impressions are made during the first few seconds of your encounter and during the last few seconds of your encounter.

1. Accept the card, look at it, and read every word that's written on it.
2. Flip it over to see if anything is printed on the back. Sometimes, organizations print their mission statement on the back of a business card; sometimes what's printed on the back is in a different language that gives you great insight as to where this person is doing business and/or traveling to.
3. As you're reading their card, be sincerely interested. Show emotion, raise your eyebrows, tilt your head.
4. Take the card and place it in a place of prominence and honor, such as an expensive cardholder, gold or silver, and in

like-new condition will work just fine. Do not shove your prospect's business card in your pocket, purse, or briefcase.

5. Always thank your prospect for his or her card.
6. Avoid, at almost any cost, handing your prospect your business card. (I'll explain why in just a moment.)

There are a few other preparatory points to remember when it comes to making a good entrance. Ready?

Never put your cell phone number or pager number, or your home number, on your business card. If possible, make sure that your business card has plenty of white space, and uses as few words as possible. (Again, you'll see why in a moment.) Consider investing the time and money necessary in a few essential gifts that should prominently feature your company's logo. (A pen that's a yellow highlighter on one end and a pen on the other, for example, or a nice executive pen, or a penlight.)

Your *exit* from your prospect's office/cube/personal workspace is an equally critical part of making a great, lasting, and memorable first impression. As you ready yourself to leave your prospect's office, you should:

1. Present your logo-sized gift to your prospect. (That fancy pen is for the prospect, not for you!)
2. Ask final questions that will invite the prospect to end your visit on a high note, or to extend your stay.
3. Present your prospect with your business card.

Here's how I suggest your card, gift giving take place. Let's break it down for each of the four players that you have the choice to call on. (*Note:* The operative word here is *choice.*)

For the Recommender

"Sorry—I almost forgot. Here's my card. And let me jot my cell phone number down on the back just in case you need any further information" (After you jot down your number with the pen/ highlighter with your logo on it, say:) *"Here, why don't you keep this, it might come in handy to highlight this weekend's [college/ professional, baseball/tennis/swiming/soccer] games. By the way,*

the next time we get together, I would love to hear the story of how you [received the best suggestion of the month award]."

For the Influencer

"Before I go, let me give you my business card. And let me jot down my pager number and the number of my [systems engineer]. If you ever have a question, don't hesitate to call. And we just got these handy penlights . . . would you like one?" (I've yet to meet an Influencer who didn't love this kind of stuff.) *"During our next meeting, I would like to understand how you were able to [design/invent/create/solve] your [network] performance issues in such a progressive way in such a short time."*

For the Decision Makers

"Here's my business card . . ." (Just as your contact reaches to take it, pull it back and say:) *"Oh, just a second."* (Now, take out that nice executive pen with your organization's logo.) *"Let me jot down my cell phone number just in case you ever need to reach me in a hurry."* (Hand your card and the pen to the Decision Maker and say:) *"Here, why don't you keep this pen—and when it comes time for us to begin our business relationship, would you do me the honor of using it to sign our agreement?"* (Then say:) *"The next time we get together, I would like for you to tell me how you personally led your team to [increase revenues in such a difficult economic time]."*

For the Approver

"Here's my business card . . ." (Just as your contact reaches to take it, pull it back and say:) *"Oh, just a second."* (Now, take that nice executive pen with your organization's logo and sign the back of the card with something like: 'To your continued success!' Then hand your card and the pen to the Approver and say:) *"Here, why don't you keep this pen as a small token of my appreciation for your time. The next time we meet, I'd love for you to tell me the story behind you founding [the company name]."*

> Signing your business card validates your personal commitment to customer satisfaction.

True Story

Of the 80 or so salespeople in the audience of a seminar that I was conducting for the largest telecommunications company in the world, one raised her hand and said: *"Signing your business card at the end of your first appointment sounds, well . . . hokey."*

Please understand that I am *not* suggesting that you hand "someone" your card. What I am suggesting is that you hand the *Approver* your signed business card.

At any rate, this participant didn't buy into what I was saying. At the time, I thought to myself: Hey, not every new idea is right for everyone. Several weeks later I got a call from a salesperson on a cell phone. "Tony," the voice said, "I met you at a seminar in Chapel Hill. I decided to use your business card signing idea and asked the Approver about how she started her company—and I can't believe what happened. She signed my contract on the first call! This is a $6,500 a month deal. The biggest one I've ever landed. She said she never experienced a salesperson with such interest in her business."

It's worth a shot, wouldn't you agree?

DO LOGO GIFTS REALLY DELIVER CUSTOMERS? TWO TRUE STORIES

At the time, the company I was selling "engineering computers" for, Hewlett Packard, didn't see the value in having a booth at the Association of Electrical Engineers national convention being held in San Diego—which was right smack in the middle of my sales territory. So I joined the association and volunteered to manage the registration booth. No one likes this job, because you have to get there early and stay late. You must be present to meet all of the registered guests. Can you guess what each person attending the convention saw when they first arrived? Yep—my face, and my computer system registering them and printing out name badges. They also got a neat little key-chain with a flashlight built into it with my company's logo on it.

Cost of logo gift give-away:	$1.87 per/attendee
Cost of my time:	Three days meeting, greeting, and collecting names, addresses, and phone numbers

Payoff: Tens of thousands of dollars in new business for HP and a nice commission on that revenue for me.

Another time, the company I was selling "manufacturing inventory control" software for didn't see the value in having a booth at the Association of Manufacturing Material Managers convention. So I volunteered to be in charge of activities for the spouses of the attendees. While everyone else was attending meetings and sessions, I was out sightseeing with the wives and husbands. They loved every minute and every outing. It was during the springtime and it rained a lot, so each person got a complementary collapsible umbrella . . . a small keepsake of our time together. Of course, it had my organization's logo on it with my personal 800 number engraved on the handle:

Make sure your logo becomes your silent sales partner.

Cost of "logo" give-away:	$6.50 per spouse
Cost of my time:	Three days (of having fun)
Payoff:	Tens of thousands of dollars in new business revenue and a nice commission on that revenue for me.

FROM COACH STEVE

CRITICAL SALES SUCCESS STEPS—STEP 2:
PICTURE YOUR FUTURE IN SALES

At the end of Chapter 10, I asked you to define a broad look at your life and future so that you could put in perspective your sales career. Most likely, you described many achievements or experiences you intend to have become reality that also required financial resources. Obviously, as a sales professional, you are perfectly positioned to generate substantial financial reward, as well as position yourself for tremendous opportunity in heading up companies of your own, starting your own business, training or managing other professionals, and so on.

(continued)

Reread the statements that you wrote in Step 1 of the Critical Sales Success Steps and add anything else that has come to mind since that time. Then, on another page, write the same type of description of how you want your future in sales to "turn out." Don't limit yourself here. If you see yourself as an account manager for the next 20 years, that is great—but if you have aspirations to lead other salespeople, build a company, run for mayor, or anything else . . . write it down! You see, all careers have a sales component. Every successful company or community leader in our marketplace will tell you that they either started in sales or wish they had more sales experience.

Define your future in a statement or two that vividly describes how your success in selling will evolve to new greater and more exciting achievements. Detail the financial and career impact of these accomplishments. Put down actual annual earnings or financial accumulations that will allow you to experience the richness of life you described in Step 1. This will be an important backdrop in defining the most productive ways to apply Tony's golden insights you are working yourself through in this book. We'll come back to that later, so for now let's get back to Tony's training.

14

PRESENTING YOUR IDEAS WITH CONVICTION

If you yourself are not totally convinced that you and your product are worthy of the second appointment and the eventual sale, you should not expect to win either the second appointment or the sale.

I strongly believe that the lack of positive convictions is the biggest single reason that we salespeople don't make the sale. Perhaps you thought it was the prospect not being "interested" in your product, service, or solution? Or not having the budget? Or the competition beating you out? Or political issues? Or problem(s) with your products? Not so!

The real origin of all these reasons not to buy resides with *you and I*—with our conviction (or lack of same) for what we sell. Like it or not, we project our convictions onto our prospects and everyone else around us.

To learn how to be convincing—both to yourself and to your prospects—you'll have to learn where the power of your own convictions come from. Convictions are formed from two forces: your opinions and your beliefs:

- *An opinion* is a view or notion, a particular judgment held or expressed. Opinions can fall short of positive knowledge. An opinion could be a combination of unproven or proven facts and ideas. It's certainly possible to have one or more opinions on the same topics; it's also very acceptable to change your opinions, or to have no opinion on a certain subject whatsoever.

- *A belief* is your thought, confidence, and trust as to your reality—your answer to the question, "What is true?" Beliefs are based on past real experiences, on generalizations, on conjecture, or on a combination of one or more of these elements. Once a belief is obtained, it's generally held to be true and rarely challenged or changed. Sometimes, we are tempted to defend our beliefs to the bitter end . . . even when there may be no factual basis for the belief in question.

Of the two, it's probably most important to understand your own beliefs. The beliefs we have affect the quality of our lives and our overall state of being. Beliefs form the basis for how we look at the world and everything in it. Our beliefs affect our actions and how we feel physically at any given moment. Countless experiments and tests have proven that once our minds form a belief, our bodies follow that belief, even if that reaction is not proper, common, predicted, or logical.

> Change your beliefs. Change your life.

In short, our beliefs affect our ability to sell. It's possible to change any belief. (Note that I didn't say it was *easy,* but it is possible!)

Beliefs are changed by introducing new information from a powerful, respected, and/or creditable source. Haven't you ever believed differently—and perhaps against your normal belief system—when you were in a crowd than you would have when you were alone?

Sometimes it doesn't take more than witnessing the behavior of other people for a belief to be installed in our brains. Think of the beliefs that people had, say, 30 years ago about whether people of African American heritage could serve as attractive role models, sports heroes, or movie stars. Nowadays, the best golfer on the planet is of African American lineage—Tiger Woods. For that matter, one of the most popular rap artists is Caucasian—Eminem. So much for beliefs about racial roles in society.

Once a new belief is present, our entire identities react powerfully, and often automatically. Of course anyone of any race can be a great golfer, or secretary of state, or a CEO, or perform in any other role. We've seen the evidence, and we know it's true. As a matter of fact, it's always been true.

The power of beliefs can have physical implications, as well as mental, emotional, and social implications. Several years ago, a group of air travelers were in flight from Los Angeles to Narita, Japan. About four hours from their destination, several passengers became violently ill. Before this ordeal was over, more than a hundred passengers also became ill, and at least 50 were take from the Narita airport by ambulance—in full view of millions of Japanese viewers via live television broadcasts on the major Japanese networks.

The illness eventually was traced to food poisoning. But here's why I'm telling you this: Many passengers who had *not* eaten any spoiled food became temporarily ill! All that was needed for them to get sick was compelling visual evidence supporting the belief that there was something wrong with the food. A few passengers on the plane actually were getting sick from tainted food. Other passengers sitting close by asked the flight attendants (an authority figure) what was wrong. The immediate and truthful response provided the social proof: "It was something they ate."

As the word spread, so did the number of passengers who became "ill." In essence, they were so convinced that they, too, had eaten spoiled food that they fell ill.

Some passengers felt ill for a good reason: They actually ate the spoiled food. As these passengers displayed symptoms of stomach cramps, nausea, and vomiting, there was a commotion. People pushed call buttons, flight attendants rushed up and down the aisles, and the captain announced that the "situation" was under control and passengers should not be concerned. The announcement, and the use of the loaded word "situation," actually did just the opposite. Who wants to be in a situation on an airplane?

When a healthy passenger asked a flight attendant what the ill passengers had eaten, her (erroneous) reply "the beef" triggered the next wave of "ill" passengers!

The power of suggestion is immensely important when it comes to forming and supporting beliefs. In this case, the *debilitating* belief "I've just been poisoned."

Hearing a story like this one should make you wonder what might happen if you and I were to decide to *build* beliefs that supported us. What would our lives be like if we proactively and selectively sought and harnessed information and knowledge from a creditable source—and presented it to ourselves first . . . and then our prospects.

If you and I were to get into such a habit, we would schedule more appointments and close more sales.

YOUR CONVICTIONS MUST BE CONVINCING

If you're going to master the art of getting the second appointment (and making the sale), you must first have an *unshakable* conviction about what you represent. That means *believing* in what you sell.

> Forming new convictions will guarantee your second appointment and making the sale in two calls.

It is often said that our actions speak louder than our words. If you believe in that statement, then you'll want to take action on the following commitments. Each is a hallmark of salespeople who develop strong, positive convictions about their products, services, and solutions:

- *Be sure you are selling something you love and can get excited about.* Passion is very convincing. It's what's called "selling from the heart." Perhaps this is why telesalespeople who work for fund-raising organizations like the American Diabetes Association and the American Cancer Association have the highest "call to revenue" ratios. People who take those jobs tend to have or develop strong personal convictions about the cause, and they're able to quickly get their prospect to a state of raised emotion. As a result, they get more positive responses over the course of a given day than other telesales folks.

- *Sell what you would purchase yourself.* If you had the need, would *you* buy that software system you're selling? Be sure you can answer that question honestly with a "yes."
- *If humanly possible, buy whatever it is you're selling.* If you sell Corvettes, you *should* be driving one! Suppose the prospect who is getting ready to spend $65,000 asks: "Which one of these Corvettes is yours?" What's going to happen if your response is: "None, I drive a Geo Metro." Or (perhaps worse yet): "None, I drive a BMW."
- *Own stock in the company you work for.* Let's face it. Stock options are cool, and they take on a personal meaning when you exercise them. Stock ownership in the company that employs you is a great selling advantage; mentioning your status as a stockholder shows your prospect that you are accountable and that you have a stake in making sure they're satisfied with what they're about to purchase.
- *Know your organization's top brass.* Building Equal Business Stature and Business Rapport with Approvers is much easier when you're in the know about the individuals that run your company. You should, at the very least, know what organization the person came from, what boards of directors they "sit" on, what college or university he or she graduated from, what philanthropic causes he or she participates in, how he or she participates in achieving your organization's goals, and how he or she defines customer service.

EIGHT HABITS OF HIGHLY COMMITTED SALESPEOPLE

By my count, there are eight habits that salespeople with the highest levels of conviction display. Which ones do you already have and which ones need reinforcement?

1. *Show up on time.* Time is a precious commodity for all of your prospects, no matter what their title happens to be. If

you waste the other person's time by being late, you'll undercut any later message you try to send about your commitment to helping the other person achieve his or her goals.

2. *Ask for favors only after you've earned the right to do so.* Deliver the results first . . . then ask for help if you must. This is a way of life whenever you're interacting with anyone of great influence and authority.

3. *Do what you say you'll do.* Nothing builds credibility faster than doing (at least) everything you make a commitment to do. In fact, your goal must be to *exceed* expectations. You can use this simple mantra to get the right message to your brain so you'll always exceed your prospect's expectations: "In order to succeed, I must exceed." Once you've indoctrinated yourself with this philosophy, you can continue to bring new ideas for achievement to the doorstep of your prospects and customers.

4. *Do the tasks that no one else does or wants to do.* When it comes time for the Approver to approve your sale, you want to be viewed as a "must have" team player—not as someone who raises a hand timidly and says, "Me, too, please."

5. *Demonstrate your commitment to continual self-improvement.* Never give your prospect (or anyone else) any reason to assume that you've become intellectually, emotionally, or physically stagnant. Show your commitment to growth in all areas of life. In particular, keep up with your customer's industry. You can't be committed to delivering results in this area if you don't know its specifics.

6. *Be optimistic.* Always be upbeat when in the presence of your prospects and customers (or, come to think of it, anyone else). Displaying this winning attitude increases the chance that, when times get tough, your prospects and customers will call on you before they call on anyone else.

7. *Dress for success.* Personal image is important, especially in the eyes of the Approver. That means it should be to you, too. Invest (sensibly) in outfits that make you look and feel like a million bucks. Just make sure you use the right clothing

to inspire higher levels of confidence *and* achievement—not as a place to hide.

8. *Be a team player.* Individuals with high levels of conviction know that there is no "I" in the word *team.* One great way to demonstrate your credentials as a team player is by instinctively giving credit to the appropriate members of the Approver's team.

Having a strong conviction about what you sell takes a sustained effort. It doesn't happen automatically. If you follow the steps that I've outlined, you will, over time, build the ability to convey your message with passion and commitment.

> Take care of your team! Share your wins with *them.* Put the spotlight on *their* desk when you make a sale.

DON'T GET CARRIED AWAY BY YOUR CONFIDENCE (A TRUE STORY)

Confidence during the first meeting is great . . . but don't let all that conviction and personal power convince you that you can somehow score points by putting down others in the prospect's organization. This is a tactic that is likely to backfire, as my own experience demonstrates.

My confidence was soaring at the completion of a two-hour facility tour. I could tell that everyone knew that our new factory data collection system would be a perfect fit! Our host, the vice president of operations, excused himself for a moment, leaving Steve, my systems engineer, and me alone. Steve and I joked about the abysmal condition of the customer's data center and the messy wiring job connecting the 100 plus terminals that we would soon be replacing. When the VP returned, he thanked us warmly for our time, said he was looking forward to our forthcoming proposal, and assured us that he liked what we had to say about his operations. Then he asked, "Did you have any questions?"

Like the (overconfident) fool I was, I smiled broadly and said, "Yes, I've got a question. Who did that mess of a wiring job in your data center?"

There was an awkward pause. The VP stared at me. I had just lost the sale, only I didn't know that yet.

Finally, the VP said: "My son."

PATIENCE IS A (SALES) VIRTUE!

Here are a few tips to build your level of understanding and patience with your prospects and customers. Actually, the following four steps will also help you with other areas in your life—with your children, partners, spouses, aging parents, and friends:

1. *Pick your cause carefully.* Ask yourself: "How many of my prospect's and/or customer's causes have I taken on in the past year that I shouldn't have?" Before you jump into a sinking boat ask: "Can I actually improve this situation? Have I successfully improved similar situations before? What will happen if my involvement makes this situation worse?"
2. *Finish what you start.* Everyone respects individuals who finish what he or she starts and individuals who refuse to take on any task that they know they can't finish. Look around . . . what's left undone in your professional environment? Clearing the clutter will give you more time to be patient with what matters.
3. *Remember: Timing is everything.* There is a season for everything in sales (and in life) till the soil, plant, water, fertilize, harvest. Skipping steps never works. And trying to accelerate the process doesn't either, which brings me to my next point.
4. *Don't take short cuts.* Certain values and steps must never be compromised. Ill-advised departures from core values and processes come with big price tags. Short-term benefits never outweigh long-term consequences.

I am working constantly on developing more patience. That's why I can say from experience that the four steps I just shared with you work!

FROM COACH STEVE

CRITICAL SALES SUCCESS STEPS—STEP 3:
DEFINE THE "DELTA"

At the end of the last chapter, you created a vivid picture of what you want your sales career to produce—personally, financially, and from a career perspective. There is likely a difference between that picture and how you might define where you are currently in your sales career. Now if there is BIG gap between where you are and where you want to go—I say "terrific!" The bigger your ideas for achievement, the more opportunity, velocity, and excitement are in store for you. But without a plan to make those spectacular things happen in life, you're just wishin' and hopin'.

Pull out your special notebook or paper that you have set aside to work through the Critical Sales Success Steps and ask yourself, "What are the specific things that I must accomplish, master, or learn to make the picture in Step 2 a reality?" This list is the "delta," or "difference," between where you are and where you want to be.

To make sure your list is complete:

➢ Go back through the notes you have made on Tony's ideas and pull out the things that you know will make the biggest difference in your sales success.

➢ Look at the skills and habits that your peers or competitors possess that you know you need work on to be more successful in selling.

➢ Quantify what you are earning versus what you want to be earning in the picture in Step 2.

➢ Specify the steps or organizational titles you will have to graduate through to attain your ultimate goal or position in your career.

Now this list is actually a list of *goals*—the foundation for your ultimate Sales Success Plan. Put it someplace handy. We'll come back to it shortly.

15

GOING PAST
THE SALE

Presenting your ideas with conviction during the first appointment is important . . . but so is knowing when (and how) to
back off. In this chapter, you get a brief overview of the best ways
to keep from "overselling" during the first meeting.

PLAY IT COOL WITH RECOMMENDERS

Overloading any Recommender with information will close the
door for all future interactions. Never proceed past your contact's
point of interest.

It's also important never to breach the trust of a Recommender.
If one of these folks ever says to you: "Don't tell anyone where you
heard this . . ." then don't!

In addition, keep away from:

- Any topic or comment that mentions your competition's
  name.
- Any topic that compares your stuff with your competitor's
  stuff.
- Any topic that downgrades or puts their current process or
  procedures in poor light.

As a general rule, the best way to leave a Recommender and ensure that the door will always be open for a return visit will be to fall short of answering all of their questions, while leaving them with a new idea of what could change for the better about any process or task they're currently doing.

PLAY IT COOL WITH INFLUENCERS

This is the one person in your prospective accounts to whom you must try to give only "need-to-know" information.

With these folks, too much information/education will *eliminate* you from any future agenda. You will have given your free training seminar . . . and the Influencer will disengage.

Avoid:

- Any topic that compares your stuff with what they happen to be using at the time.
- Any topic that questions "why" or any statement that uses the word "why" in it, such as: "Why did you choose your current . . ."
- Any statement that goes beyond the question(s) that they may have.
- Any topic that introduces "future" products that your new product development team happens to be working on.

> Don't give your competition free advertising by mentioning their name to your prospects.

"What's your 25 gigabyte drive's latency factor?" I'd heard that question so many times from Influencers who were educated on my biggest competitor's products that my answer was automatic to all and anyone who asked: "It's shorter than Acme Group's by a factor of two, and we've been able to achieve a density factor of seven times greater than their top-of-the-line drives." In this case, though, the Influencer was unfamiliar with my competition, so I heard this in response: "Oh—I didn't realize that Acme Group had a 25 gig drive." Open mouth, insert foot.

As a general rule the best way to leave a Influencer and ensure that the door will always be open for a return visit will be to answer questions with great care. I believe that the answer to any Influencer's question should:

1. Be broken into time segments. The length of each segment's answer should not exceed the time it took for the question to be asked.
2. Be spoken in parts if need be: "Let me answer your question in two parts . . ." Then add between each part with a checking comment: "Did that help?" or: "Is that helpful" or: "What else would you need?" Avoid at all costs asking: "Did that answer your question?" (No matter what you said, the answer will always be, "Not really.")
3. Be spoken slowly.
4. Let the Influencer interject their comments and/or other additional questions.

Empathy is also important when dealing with Influencers. (And with Recommenders, for that matter.) Acknowledge where this person is—without necessarily agreeing or claiming to have been in the same situation. Here's how to do it:

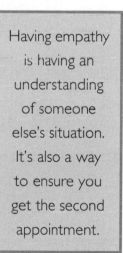

Having empathy is having an understanding of someone else's situation. It's also a way to ensure you get the second appointment.

1. Be a sounding board. Allow Influencers to bounce their feelings off you while you assume a nonjudgmental, noncritical manner.
2. Don't ask too many closed-ended questions in a row.
3. Don't become angry, hurt, or upset at anything Influencers might say to you. (This is particularly important when Influencers are telling you of an experience they've had with your products, services, and solutions in the past.)

PLAY IT COOL WITH DECISION MAKERS

It is extremely important to do more listening than talking with Decision Makers. The key to this is to put your ego aside and become an active listener and an honest "taker" of advice. That means often you'll hear comments and statements that you don't agree with or want to hear.

For example, it's quite conceivable that a Decision Maker could say something like this: "I like what I see, but I must tell you that at this point I am doubtful that we could take advantage of what you and your organization has to offer for at least another year."

Fight the urge to respond with: "Ms. Importanta, your knowledge-based workers are operating at reduced levels of effectiveness, which by our estimates is causing a 25 percent increase in your cost of sales. Our ideas are proven and will quickly eliminate this situation and get your cost of sales back on track. Why don't you let me put together a proposal?"

All you're going to get in response is: "I'm aware of that. What I'm telling you is we're not ready to do business with you."

Instead, say something like this: "You obviously have a good reason for saying that . . . could you please share with me what it is?"

Here's what you might get back: "We're getting ready to acquire a competitor and once that's over, I'll be in a position to implement a larger version of what we've been discussing." Now, that's much better isn't it?

As a general rule, the best way to leave a Decision Maker and ensure that the door will always be open for a return visit will be to leave your Decision Maker wanting more. Specifically, don't discuss:

- Any topic that puts any of their team members or processes in question of their performance.
- Any topic that questions their influence and/or authority.
- Anything of a confidential nature about any of your other customers or your own organization.

Last but not least—don't overstate your capacities and your ability to perform.

PLAY IT COOL WITH APPROVERS

Remember that it's the Approver's show. It's okay for the Approver to come to conclusions—but *you* don't get to come to conclusions during this meeting.

Listen carefully and stick to the following goals during the initial meeting:

> It's okay to leave an appointment with your prospect wanting more. It ups your chances of getting the second appointment.

1. *Find out:* What's this Approver's level of loyalty to their organization's current source of supply that you're wanting to replace?
2. *Find out:* Will your ideas/products/services and solutions cross departmental/divisional lines?
3. *Find out:* What is this Approver's timing for each of their strategic initiatives?
4. *Find out:* Who in the Approver's organization has the task of implementing the tactical initiatives?

As a general rule, the best way to leave an Influencer and ensure that the door will always be open for a return visit will be to ask a question that is thought-provoking and yet does not threaten or challenge the Approver's ego, power, control, and/or authority, and that invites him or her to *tell you exactly what to do next.*

Here are some examples of what I mean. I strongly suggest that you use some variation of one or more of the following questions near the end of your first meeting with the Approver:

- "At this time, before we move forward and your team spends their valuable time with me let me ask: What are you looking for in a business relationship?"
- "From what we know so far, your organization's loyalty to its current source of supply is unintentionally costing you [as much as 11 percent excess shipping costs]. What's the best way to take our level of involvement to the next level to see if we can help your lower that number between now and let's say the end of the [first fiscal quarter]?"
- "If we assume for a moment that you're interested in a business relationship with my organization, what's the best way to explore all of the possibilities in the shortest period of time?"

- "We suspect that our ideas will be able to [increase your overall revenue generating abilities] what normally must take place in your organization to put similar ideas to use?"
- "The one fact we do know is that we've helped similar organizations accomplish similar results. What else can you share with me that would get us closer to understanding if we can create even greater results for your enterprise between now and the end of the [first fiscal quarter]?"
- "It's been our past experience that we can [cut nonvalue expense from HR budgets] which may or may not work for you. How could we gain an audience with your [HR] Decision Makers?"
- "Each one of our customers is unique and because of that it's difficult to make an estimate of your exact results with our [production ideas]. Who on your team of [manufacturing experts] would you like for me to continue this conversation with between now and the end of this business day?"

NOW, YOU GIVE IT A TRY

Before you continue on to the next chapter, stop here and, on a separate sheet of paper, write out your own "don't go past the sale" questions for each of the players.

FROM COACH STEVE

CRITICAL SALES SUCCESS STEPS—STEP 4:
DEFINE OBSTACLES AND OPPORTUNITIES

In Step 3 of your Critical Sales Success Steps, you came up with the *delta* between where you are and where you want to be from a professional sales perspective. This ended up being a list of goals for future career success. I recommend that you keep this list "alive" by looking at it periodically and adding and checking off items as you learn more and develop as a sales professional. Also, don't forget to keep it handy as you finish this book—Tony has left the best for last and you will

---

likely discover additional insights on what it will take to achieve your ultimate career successes.

Meanwhile, let's begin building a detailed plan for sales success. On the way to accomplishing each of the items you defined in Step 3, there will be both opportunities and obstacles. Opportunities will be those resources or circumstances that, if you were to capitalize on with intention, you could leverage to accelerate your way to achieving that goal or objective. For example:

> ➢ What tools, skills or talents are you not currently using in your sales process that, if used effectively would assist you in accomplishing your goal?
> ➢ Who (peers, superiors, company execs, friends, customers, etc.) can you use to help you achieve each goal and what specifically would you ask them to do for you?
> ➢ What hard and soft resources could you leverage or utilize that you know you are not currently taking advantage of (time in each day, time in each week, current financial resources that could be invested better, etc.)?

Next, make the same list of Obstacles. For most, this is a bit easier but also a list that we avoid the most. You know yourself better than anyone else. Fess up . . . what are the things that you know right now could stand in the way of your future success?

> ➢ Bad habits.
> ➢ Bad thinking.
> ➢ Fear.
> ➢ Limited resources.
> ➢ Perceived limitations.
> ➢ Self sabotage.

List all of these things without concern with how we will address them. That's coming in the next coaching session.

16

NEEDS AND WANTS

There are three very different situations you will encounter during the first appointment (or, for that matter, during subsequent appointments).

1. *Your prospect doesn't really see the need or doesn't really want what you happen to be selling* but is willing to grant you a first and/or second appointment to talk anyway. In this situation, you won't be making any sale.
2. *Your prospect sees the need and wants what you happen to be selling—and he or she will grant you a first and second appointment but . . .* These are the situations that boast a big "but"—your contact does not have the influence and/or authority and/or approval power to buy what you happen to be selling. In this situation, you may or may not end up making any sale.
3. *Your prospect sees the need and wants what you happen to be selling and will grant you a first and second appointment . . . and they have influence and authority and can approve the purchase.* These are your "high-percentage" shots.

QUESTIONS TO ASK YOURSELF

Many salespeople are big on conducting needs assessments, but wonder why they end up intimidating the people whose needs they're supposedly assessing. Consider the following important issues before you try to conduct any needs assessment during the first appointment, or indeed during any appointment:

1. *Do you ask questions in a way that proves to the "askee" that you sincerely care?* This is what prospects (and everyone else) want most of all. Each player in the company you want to sell to wants to be served and do business with someone who truly cares. Therefore, when uncovering needs and wants, the most important message that we can communicate is that we care. If you care, and show it, you will be forgiven almost any mistake or error. But, perhaps more important, you will be granted a second appointment and most likely make the sale.

2. *Do you really listen to the answers of your questions?* Let's face it, everyone needs to be heard and everyone wants to be understood. The quickest path to understanding the needs and wants of your prospects will be honest, active listening. It's been my personal experience that when I have clearly demonstrated that I have understood my prospect, I have won the sale even in situations where my product was not the best fit or price.

> There is only one situation that will ensure you make the sale in two calls: Your prospect has the influence and authority to make the decision *and* they have the approval power to buy.

3. *Do you behave in a professional manner at all times?* Would you let an attorney represent you or your family if you felt that he or she was likely to use unprofessional standards? Of course not! You and I have a similar obligation to uphold high professional standards in our work. That means never pretending to know someone when you don't, never applying high-pressure techniques or putting a customer or prospect on the spot, never rambling on, never exaggerating, never attempting flattery by making false statements, and never undertaking any action that is inconsistent with your own sense of integrity and morality.

4. *Do your prospects feel in control when you're with them?* We all have the need to be in control of our own destiny. No one likes to feel manipulated or

forced into doing anything. The best way to *control* the outcome of any sales situation is to influence the outcome. The best way to influence the outcome is to ask the right guiding questions in a way that shows that you sincerely care. In other words, go back to item 1.

STUDYING NEEDS

Each of the four categories of individuals in your prospective and existing accounts is faced with different challenges and initiatives; each has different needs and wants. Furthermore, as time passes in your sales process, their needs and wants can and will change. With all of these dynamics going on, you'll be able to count on one factor that will rarely change—and that's the person's personality style. Here is my best advice on uncovering the needs of the people you'll be working with.

UNCOVERING NEEDS WITH THE APPROVER (TYPICALLY A DRIVER PERSONALITY)

When uncovering the needs and wants of an Approver, you must always keep in mind that these folks are brief, direct, and to-the-point. They'll have little patience for questions that do not directly address their needs. Therefore, it's best to blend any questions that you might have with information that the Approver cannot get from any other source. Along the same lines, we should never request any information from an Approver that is available from anyone else.

Other pointers on uncovering needs when dealing with these folks:

- Be fast paced, to the point, and extremely organized when uncovering their needs (or doing anything else in their presence).
- Know the Approver's industry.
- Avoid any language or terminology that is unfamiliar to the Approver.
- Aim all of your questions at the heart of each issue.

- Ask direct questions in a practical manner and always use simple language.
- Avoid "doom and gloom" types of questions. ("In this down economy, what's your opinion of . . .")
- Always assume that they have knowledge. Use statements like: "As you know . . ." "As you're aware of . . ." Avoid statements like: "Did you know . . ." "Let me tell you . . ."
- Take short cuts whenever possible and cut out steps or descriptions whenever possible.
- If you have a list of 10 items, let the Approver know that you're skipping some to get to the bottom line faster.

UNCOVERING NEEDS WITH THE DECISION MAKER (TYPICALLY AN EXPRESSIVE PERSONALITY)

You'll recall from earlier in the book that we'll be looking for the Decision Maker to sponsor our ideas and our product, service, and solutions. You'll also recall that their job as it relates to your sales process is to say "yes"—and to get the Approver's go ahead.

Ultimately, you must make sure that it is very clear to the Decision Maker that your ideas will totally support his or her current goals, plans, and objectives. During your efforts to uncover the needs of Decision Makers, don't be surprised if something extraordinary happens such as the person sharing personal aspirations. Whenever this happens—whenever your Decision Maker starts talking about his or her life, career, or personal long-term goals— pay attention! This is a flashing neon sign saying, "Here's what you need to address in order to get me excited about working with you."

If at all possible, tie *all* of your questions about helping the Decision Maker professionally to personal goals or anecdotes he or she shares with you.

Here are some other pointers to keep in mind when uncovering the needs ands wants of the expressive Decision Maker:

- This person's favorite topic will most likely be past accomplishments and future goals; when in doubt, ask about these.
- Keep every statement you make in balance. Illustrate the upside *and the downside* of all of your ideas. It's best to set the

stage with the possibilities of all risks first. Being realistic and optimistically truthful will gain the respect of the Decision Maker.

> It's safe to say that personal goals and professional goals are the same with a Decision Maker.

- When talking about current needs, ask how the "now" situation compares to "past" and possible "future" needs. Decision Makers like to think in terms of longevity of your relationship with them.
- Image and recognition are critically important to these people; unlike many Approvers, Decision Makers typically like knowing what others are doing and have done in a similar situation. As a result, third-party referrals worked into the discussions about their needs will yield more favorable results.
- Bending and changing the rules is a popular pastime with Decision Makers. "Standard" anything will be of little appeal to these people.
- Ask questions that will give Decision Makers the opportunity to give you their advice.
- Always take their advice and follow their directions. Decision Makers will not sponsor you or your ideas if they feel you're not allowing them to lead you.

UNCOVERING NEEDS WITH THE INFLUENCER (TYPICALLY AN ANALYTIC PERSONALITY)

Reminder: Spending too much time with Influencers is bad for your commission totals.

I am not suggesting that we ignore or avoid these folks; I am suggesting that we limit our time with them and make sure that we are embracing multiple levels of contact and take equal time with people at the other levels.

Whenever you're uncovering the needs and wants of your analytic Influencer, keep these tips in mind:

- Be totally prepared. Have all of your questions and statements written down ahead of time.

- Make sure your questions are logical, practical, and based in the Influencer's current reality.
- As you uncover the Influencer's needs, make sure that you're also uncovering their wealth of knowledge and expertise.
- Provide documentation as to how and why your ideas apply to their needs.
- Don't probe into their personal agenda or reasoning.
- Don't doubt your contact's knowledge or attempt to correct him or her.

UNCOVERING NEEDS WITH THE RECOMMENDER
(OFTEN AN AMIABLE PERSONALITY)

You'll recall, worker bees of all sorts and titles will fall into this category. You'll find that uncovering the needs of these individuals will be the most encouraging of all the other players. Why? Because you'll immediately see the "fit" of your products, services, and solutions to what they need. As a result, you'll be tempted to try to sell to these individuals but by this point in the book, you know how big a mistake that is, right?

Always remember that your job is to explore with these folks. Here are some other tips to keep you on-track when uncovering the needs and wants of Recommenders:

- Take time to draw Recommenders out. Any attempt to uncover their needs must be done so in a gentle, friendly, warm manner.
- Ask questions that show Recommenders how your ideas will support, simplify, or stabilize their current procedures, processes, and work relationships.
- Don't ask Recommenders to compromise their position by asking any questions that have the chance of getting an "I can't tell you that" response.
- Don't expect Recommenders to deliver any bad news to you—like the fact that the budget you're trying to tap into is frozen. It's not that Recommenders are trying to undermine you, it's just that they don't like to hurt anyone's feelings.

- Always end each question that you ask Recommenders with something like this: "Is this an important [concern, issue, situation, parameter, capability, area] for you personally?"
- If you ask a question, and the Recommender doesn't have an answer, don't pressure your contact or put him or her on the spot.

WHAT HAPPENS NEXT?

There are two steps you should plan to take that will help you to set up the second appointment. They are:

1. Thank-you note and an acknowledgment of what was discovered (Timing: Immediate).
2. A detailed *gap analysis;* discussion of where the organization is today compared to where they want to be in the future (Timing: Within one week).

Let's look briefly at how you can handle these steps.

Thank-You Note and Acknowledgment

In this click-and-point world we're all selling in, it becomes critically important to create an immediate written "touch-point" after any and all encounters we have with our prospects and customers. Be it over the telephone or in-person, there is no replacement for the benefit of a handwritten, original, and signed thank-you note.

Let me emphasize that you must deliver it or send this message *immediately* (that is, within 24 hours) after you conclude your encounter, meeting, appointment, or conversation. Any longer, and its impact and value is diminished.

For the Recommender, use your signature and a tag-line like: "It was a pleasure meeting you." If at all possible, include, along with your signature, the signature of your service technician, head of customer service, or customer training department; this person should say something like: "looking forward to

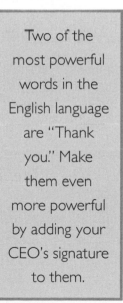

Two of the most powerful words in the English language are "Thank you." Make them even more powerful by adding your CEO's signature to them.

servicing you," or "looking forward to sharing our product with you," or "looking forward to having you in one of my operator training classes."

For the Influencer, use your signature and this tag-line: "Thanks for your insights." If at all possible, include the signature of your head designer, scientist, or the creator of your product, service, or solution, who will write something like: "I'll look forward to your ideas and insights about our product," or, "looking forward to meeting you soon."

For the Decision Maker, use your signature and this tag-line: "I look forward to serving you and your team." If at all possible, use the signature of your vice president of sales with something like: "my team of experts awaits your direction and coaching," or "looking forward to brainstorming with you personally."

For the Approver, use your signature and this tag-line: "To your continued success." If at all possible, include the signature of your CEO, president, or owner, writing something like this: "Our main goal is to pay attention to the details that make a difference to you."

By the way, whenever you send a thank-you note to an Approver's personal assistant, make sure you actually address it and mail it to the Approver, not the Approver's personal assistant. At the same time, you should include a short handwritten note along the following lines for the Approver:

"Thanks for having Tommie on your team. Her guidance and insights to our understanding your future goals was extremely valuable."

Can't you just see Tommie's face as she reads the message before passing it along to the Approver? (After all, who opens the mail for the Approver?)

MIND THE GAP

The *GAP* (goal above performance) analysis is a written summary of where the organization is today compared to where they want to be in the future. This document must reach your prospect no more than one week after your first meeting.

Have you ever promised your prospect that you would send him or her something, and, for whatever reason, you totally missed the deadline? Upon remembering this, did you quickly pick up the telephone and call or did you feel embarrassed and somewhat shameful and not call? I've certainly been guilty of the latter, and the longer I waited the more embarrassed and shameful I became.

Well, here's a way to *never* miss the opportunity to follow up. I develop a formal GAP document on every single first meeting/appointment. This is an important part of my sales process, one that gives me a way to move the prospect forward in knowing what I can and can't do without me personally meeting with them. This document also sets up an expectation that I can be depended on and I am a true "value-added" business ally.

The GAP analysis accurately and succinctly points out in writing to whomever you met with *your interpretation* of what you observed and where they told you they wanted to be. It explores a few of your ideas in a very general sense. It should be a formal part of your post-meeting routine.

Each GAP analysis has four parts:

1. Restatement of the problem/challenge you observed.
2. The *hint* of an idea that you've got an answer for.
3. A way for your contact to provide feedback to you.
4. A suggestion as to what your contact's next step might be and when he or she may want to take it.

You can develop a GAP analysis for anyone, of course, but I would strongly recommend that you find a way to develop one for the Decision Makers and Approvers in your target organization. Here's a sample GAP analysis I developed recently for an Approver; you may want to consider using it as a model.

• • •

Notice how this short correspondence on page 182 satisfies all of the requirements of the GAP analysis. You can send it by regular mail, fax, or via e-mail; my preference is to use all three.

Dear Mr. Benefito,

After spending three days with your new business acquisition team, it became apparent to both your team and mine that your fourth quarter goals were in jeopardy of being overachieved, which is in line with the overview you provided in your office the morning we met. Here's an immediate list of what we came up with to get back on track and satisfy your vision:

- Consider redeploying your web advertising to attract only prospects that fall within the demographics of your best customers.
- Move to a wider distribution channel and immediately weed out existing value-added resellers who are not meeting their quota.
- Train each of your remaining partners and direct salespeople on the tactics of using top-down sales techniques.
- Put in place a lead tracking system that gets hot prospects to your teams within 24 hours of acquisition.
- Bring in a web-based communication tool to improve the dispersement of best-practices advice.

At this point there are two areas we need your advice on. First, it would be helpful if you would provide your feedback directly to me as to how your would like to prioritize and/or modify this list. Second, would you like to make your existing customer care center manager available for her input as to how we can create additional revenue through an existing customer touch-point program?

I will await your direction.

To your continued success,
Tony Parinello
(800) 777-8486

WHAT ELSE GOES WITH THE GAP ANALYSIS?

Nothing but a cover letter . . . an extremely important document that we'll cover in the next chapter.

LOCK IN WHAT YOU'VE LEARNED

I invite you to participate in an e-learning exercise that I've developed based on this chapter. Visit www.gettingthesecondappointment .com and then click on Chapter 16 Online Assets. You'll get a chance to download several GAP Analyses and other valuable information along with your free trial membership of my Getting the Second Appointment Success Portal.

17

THE RULES OF CORRESPONDENCE

In crafting cover letters, e-mails, and other documents to the people in your target organization, consider the following four-step rollout plan, which I've personally field tested and can vouch for with enthusiasm:

1. Send written correspondence.
2. Call to follow up and attempt to secure your next meeting.
3. Return to step 2 six more times, or until the next meeting is set (whichever comes first).
4. Then back go to step 1.

Having established that (relatively simple) model, we are free to move on to the rules you should observe while crafting written post-first meeting messages for specific players within the organization.

A preparatory word of caution: *Every* post-meeting piece of written correspondence should pursue the following topics in the following sequence, based on the intended recipient:

Recommender: Move from functions to features.
Influencer: Move from features to functions.
Decision Maker: Move from advantages to benefits.
Approver: Move from benefits to advantages.

RECOMMENDER: WRITE FROM
FUNCTIONS TO FEATURES

You'll recall that Functionality of what you are selling is the "how it's used"—and you'll also remember that the Recommenders of the enterprise are the users of what you sell. Start with the functions, then move on to the features used to deliver those functions.

Recommenders tend to live in a "now-oriented" world because they can't stop whatever they're doing. They can't afford the luxury of stopping . . . they'll fall behind. That's why it does little good to address any concern or interest in your correspondence other than what is likely to be going on right at this moment.

> Don't bother sending any correspondence that you don't use a telephone call to follow up on.

Even if the Recommender is part of a committee formed to explore the possibility of changing a process or work flow, he or she will, by sheer force of habit, usually evaluate anything in your message based on whether or not it is likely to affect their current situation. (And by "current," I mean the pile of papers that's on the Recommender's desk right now, or the next call he or she has to take, or the shipment that's coming in this afternoon.)

Warning: Current priorities and workloads will always affect the degree of attention your message receives from the Recommender (or anyone else in the organization, for that matter). Let's say you're an industry expert (AKA a salesperson) representing a property management firm, and you already know the parameters that your Recommenders are most likely operating under. You write a letter to the site manager of a 2,500 unit complex, assuming that he or she will respond well to any idea that addresses the Functionality of specific beginning-of-the month activities like rent collection, move-ins, eviction notices, and so on. However, if you send the letter ignoring the fact it will in fact *arrive* at the beginning of the month (when you know your contact is busiest), you shouldn't be surprised if it's ignored. Better to send it in the middle of the month.

> Timing the arrival of your correspondence will greatly impact if it gets read or not!

When writing to Recommenders recruited to evaluate your product or service, be sure to:

- Write in very easy-to-understand terms.
- Offer a multitude of ideas and options.
- Use *block-diagrams* wherever possible.
- Include brief sections from your owner's manual (if you have one).
- Focus on the functionality of your products, services, and solutions.
- Provide only information that is directly related to their committee's evaluation.
- If at all possible, include a way for the Recommender to personally experience your products, services, and solutions.
- Stay away from "selling" language.
- Include a handwritten "thank you for your interest/attention" note or notation on the letter.
- Conclude with specifics about what you think should happen next in the relationship.

When developing written correspondence for a Recommender you're casually exploring—someone who isn't part of a committee—you should:

- Adopt a friendly, informal, but professional tone.
- Include casual information about the functionality of your products, services, and solutions.
- Consider including handwritten notes in the margins and Post-it notes on the pages.
- Mention information about this Recommender's personal interests.
- Include an article or other piece of information about a subject of mutual interest.

INFLUENCER: WRITE FROM FEATURES TO FUNCTIONS

Being totally aware of the rules and regulations will go a long way to getting your correspondence opened and read by the Influencer.

Typically, this means focusing first on the specifications and other details of (familiar) features, and then on what those features actually accomplish.

Suppose you're an industry expert who knows that industrial engineers will eventually be asked to evaluate of your dies and composite materials. The first impression your correspondence will make must be one of accuracy and completeness. Addressing current challenges is critical. Focus on issues like tool longevity, cutting down on process re-works, and reducing downtime of machining equipment. Putting these issues up front in your correspondence will put the Influencer's mind at ease.

> Never sell in any way, shape, or form in your correspondence to an Influencer.

When composing correspondence for Influencers, you should:

- Make absolutely sure the document is logically and technically sound, and that it does not make any assumptions or introduce any subject matter that is unfounded, unproven, or overstated.
- Include multiple pages.
- Feature a directory or table of contents.
- Include tables, charts, matrices, and comparisons.
- Use color to highlight important material or specifications.
- State fact, not fiction.
- Feature a section written by your design/development, scientific, and/or engineering division.
- Include as appendices technical articles that substantiate your data.
- Stay away from selling language.
- Pass along relevant information about your organization's ranking in the industry, along with any product or, industry awards that have been received.
- End with an open agenda. (Influencers don't like being told what to do.)

Putting together a document of this nature is a lot of work. Your product, service, and/or solution's data sheets are a great source for the information and once you get one done you'll be able to "cut and paste" any others that are for Influencers that are in the same industry. It's also a good idea to create a "carrier" for this document in the form of a file folder with a tab affixed to it so your Influencer can file and retrieve it quickly and easily. It would be very effective to include a computer disc that contains all of the contents of your correspondence and/or send a copy of your written correspondence via e-mail.

DECISION MAKER: WRITE FROM ADVANTAGES TO BENEFITS

You'll recall that Decision Makers care about the *advantages* of what you offer. Start with the advantages—the ways in which you can tailor, modify, tweak, and otherwise change one or more of the aspects of your products, services and solutions to match precisely the needs of this Decision Maker. Start your correspondence from there, and then move on to the benefits of what you sell.

> Decision Makers will need to know specifically what date and time to expect your follow-up call.

Sure, it will take a little time and effort to customize your letter, but if you don't do this, you won't have a second meeting (or a sale) to worry about. So, make the investment.

Any attachments you include must address your depth of knowledge about your ability to perform in this Decision Maker's distinctive niche. Your correspondence should include an easy way for this Decision Maker to respond back to you with his thoughts, requests, and directives.

Your letter to the Decision Maker *must* demonstrate depth of knowledge within this person's sphere of operations. It should also include:

- Mentions of relevant industry awards or accolades about customer satisfaction ratings.
- Proof of customer focus groups and the results they brought about.
- Proof of user groups and the results they brought about.

- The ratios of revenue to research and development that your organization supports.
- A request for the Decision Maker's opinion. ("My vice president of customer service and I would like to learn more about your experience with . . .")
- A time that you're going to follow up on the correspondence.

That last item is particularly important. What you write should sound pretty close to the following: "P.S. I will call your office, Tuesday, May 14 at 11:30 A.M. If this is an inconvenient time you can call me at: (800) 777-8486 between 3 and 5 P.M. Monday thru Friday to reschedule."

Yes, you'll be making the call and yes, a later chapter will cover all of the important aspects of this all-important call.

APPROVER: WRITE FROM BENEFITS
TO ADVANTAGES

Approvers (unlike just about anyone else in the organization) will read anything *at any time* that addresses their universal need of increasing share holder value.

Your correspondence to this group should start by focusing on one or more of the following benefits:

- *Revenues:* Increases performance in all divisions/product lines and market areas.
- *Efficiency:* Increases of revenue-generating employees, mission-critical employees, and mission-critical processes sustained over the period of time it takes to repay the investment made.
- *Effectiveness:* Increases of revenue-generating employees, mission-critical employees, and mission-critical processes sustained over the period of time no less than the time it takes to repay the investment made.
- *Market share protection:* Elimination of the need to win back existing customers.
- Obtaining greater add-on business from existing customer base.
- Elimination of nonvalue expense.

Once you've addressed one or more of these issues in a compelling fashion, you can focus on the customized advantages you personally bring to the table.

There are a number of important rules you must follow when composing correspondence for Approvers. These rules include:

1. Make it a quick read. (Remember, there's a big difference between a short letter and one that's a quick read; I've read plenty of short letters that were nearly impossible to read, and I'll bet you have, too.)
2. Make it no more than one page long.
3. Make it relevant to what's currently a priority in this Approver's world.
4. Make sure you use headlines and bullets effectively.
5. Make sure the Approver can easily understand it.
6. Make it easy for the Approver to forward it to one or more of his or her Decision Makers.
7. Make sure you pro-actively pick a time that you're going to follow up on the correspondence.

Again, the final element is vitally important. As with your correspondence to the Decision Maker, I strongly suggest that you use a postscript for this portion of the letter.

An example of an effective letter to an Approver appears on page 193.

Notice that this letter:

1. Provides an idea that's easy to understand and can assist in the overachievement of the Approver's goals, plans, and objectives in the near future.
2. Provides an idea about how your organization can shorten the Approver's time to realizing some aspect of number 1.
3. Offers social proof about precisely how you accomplished something similar for someone else in this Approver's niche.

The aim is to make your correspondence to this Approver so relevant to what's going on in his or her world that the recipient is not only willing to take your call, but also receptive to your ideas about what should happen next in the relationship.

PUTTING POSTAGE ON YOUR CORRESPONDENCE

When it comes to sending your correspondence, you have a few choices concerning postage. Here are my preferences:

1. *USPS, first-class letter delivery:* Still the best deal in town—reliable and inexpensive. Just be sure to allow plenty of time for internal mailroom sorting and delivery. You may want to call your prospect and let him or her know the letter's on the way.

2. *Overnight package/parcel delivery:* Expensive, but highly predictable. I suggest you only use this mode of delivery when strict deadlines are in place. Use in other situations can leave the contact wondering about your fiscal sense.

> Use more than one way to send each piece of correspondence you write.

3. *Facsimile:* I like using a fax to inform my prospects that I've just sent a first-class package their way or to send a sheet or two to update some previous document that I've sent.

4. *E-mail:* The greatest invention since the steam engine! Just don't assume that the simple fact that you *sent* it means that they *got* it. Always call or fax to confirm that your message traveled thru cyber-space correctly.

Now that our correspondence has been sent, it's time to pick up the telephone and enter the promised land by making that call we promised.

LOCK IN WHAT YOU'VE LEARNED

I invite you to participate in an e-learning exercise that I've developed based on this chapter. Visit www.gettingthesecondappointment .com and then click on Chapter 17 Online Assets. You'll get a chance to download several different types of correspondence and other valuable information.

"65 of the Fortune 100 increased earning while reducing their cost of sales by as much as 50%. Would you like to meet the team who made it possible?"
Edward Keyes, Pres

May 14, 2

Mr. Benefito
President

Dear Mr. Benefito,

During the past seven years, we have worked with 75 organizations in the banking industry. We've listened, learned, and created ideas and solutions. Collectively, we've been able to increase revenues and efficiencies while at the same time providing ways to increase shareholder value.

Are any of the following achievements on your list of goals, plans, or objectives for the balance of this calendar year? If so, the good news is that now we're ready to offer these ideas for your consideration:

- **Increased initial transaction size** up to 54%. Typically, our clients also experience a shorter time-to-revenue for these larger sales.
- **Effectiveness/efficiency enhancements** of knowledge-based workers. Our clients find that 15% of their top-line revenue was being spent in direct support of this part of their workforce. We compressed this expense to 9%.
- **Protect existing market share**—Employee and client satisfaction and retention consistently adds up to better utilization of human assets. I invite you to consider what an employee turnover of only 2% and customer churn of less than 6% does for shareholder value.

Mr. Benefito, it's obvious you know your organization better than anyone does. But what may not be so obvious is how our ideas could help you realize similar or even greater results before the end of this calendar year. If you would like to take the first step, our complete team of experts can quickly determine each and every possibility.

All the success,

Will Prosper
(760) 765-1321

P.S. I will call your office on Thursday, March 18 at 10:00 A.M. If this is an inconvenient time, please have Tommie inform me as to when I should place the call.

FROM COACH STEVE

CRITICAL SALES SUCCESS STEPS—STEP 5:
BUILD A SPECIFIC ACTION PLAN

Take a look at the list of Opportunities and Obstacles that you made at the end of Chapter 15. In this step—Step 5 of the Critical Sales Success Steps—you will simply pick out the three to five Opportunities and the three to five Obstacles that, if addressed, will make the biggest near-term impact on your career as a sales professional. Using these lists, answer the question on a separate piece of paper, "So what am I going to do about this?" As you answer that question for each item, make sure that you list the following components to a "proper" action plan:

1. Define the action item in terms that are specific and in a way that you will know if you have achieved the item or not. For example, "get better at prospecting" is a hard thing to check off a list. If you wrote, "Improve appointment ratio by 25 percent," you would be able to easily measure and complete that item.
2. Set a specific time or date deadline. Ask yourself, "By when?"

Don't worry about detailing every little thing that might address an opportunity or obstacle. The key is to define an action item or two that will get you moving toward leveraging the opportunities and clearing the obstacles. The real effort you employ may end up being more or less than what you planned, but the major "win" is that you have put yourself in motion toward addressing the key elements of sales success!

18

KEYS TO
TELEPHONE SUCCESS

I n this chapter, I'd like to look at how we use the telephone—and
at how you can increase the power and effectiveness of your
calls when it comes to scheduling more appointments with your
prospects.

GENERAL OBSERVATIONS

There are five important elements that are in your *direct control*
whenever you pick up the telephone to talk to a potential customer.
Those elements are:

1. Tone.
2. Modulation.
3. Volume.
4. Pacing.
5. Length of time you choose to speak over the phone.

Let's look at each of these elements—and how they can help
you schedule more appointments with your contacts.

Tone

First and foremost, you must to be concerned about the tone of
your voice. The tone you use will determine how easy (or difficult)

it will be for the person on the other end of the line to process your message. Contrary to popular belief, your tone can be changed. The natural, and most appealing, tone of your voice is actually the tone of your "hum"; this probably isn't the tone you habitually use during conversations. The secret to finding and using your natural voice is simply to practice a little each day by picking your favorite song and humming a bar . . . then sing that same bar. Pick the same song for several days in a row, then change the song. In next to no time, your natural voice will appear effortlessly in all of your conversations, whether on the telephone or in other situations.

Modulation

We're not looking for a "sing-song" type of presentation here, with plenty of highs and lows. What works best is to modulate your voice to the topic and emotions of your discussion. When something is important, or when you're asking a question, your modulation should vary. (If you're looking for guidance on modulation, close your eyes and listen to one of the nightly network news anchors deliver his or her text.) Generally, you'll want to raise the pitch of your voice during the last few words when asking a question and lower the pitch of your voice during the last few words when making a statement of fact.

> Your voice not your product is your most powerful sales tool.

Volume

We learned a simple principle while we were children: The more important your point is, the louder your voice should be. This is a big mistake! In a professional setting, your volume should remain *constant.* Judicious use of *silence,* or modulation of tone or pitch, is the best way to emphasize a point.

Pacing

The speed at which you speak should match the speaking speed of the person to whom you are speaking. Here are some generalizations you can use early on in the conversation, while you're trying to get a sense of the speaking speed of your contact:

- *Approvers:* Assume fastest paced delivery.
- *Decision Makers:* Assume second fastest paced delivery.
- *Recommenders:* Assume slower paced delivery.
- *Influencers:* Assume slowest paced delivery.

The higher up in the hierarchy you go, the less time you have to make your point. I always plan the pace of my monologue to suit each of the players. Let me mention here that the world-class sales trainers I've met over the years are in profound disagreement about how much time salespeople have before the person on the other end of the phone loses interest and disengages from the call (either mentally or physically). My estimate is that you and I have a meager eight seconds, whether speaking on the phone or in person, to get to the point and get a reaction. That may seem like a very short time, but try this experiment: The next time you are driving and you stop at a red light, wait until the traffic builds up behind you. Then, when the light turns green, *wait eight seconds* before you hit the accelerator. You'll soon be convinced that eight seconds is a very long time indeed!

A final general note: Avoid, at all costs, making your calls from cell phones (they're dangerously close to inaudible) or using headsets, even an expensive one (they're only marginally better).

On the Phone with the Approver

The reason I'm starting with the Approver is that it's my firm belief if you want to get a second appointment and/or make the sale in two calls, you'll want start at the top of the organization and work downward. (But you knew that.)

Here are the principles I've learned from experience to follow during phone exchanges with the Approver:

- *Never commit anything, especially your opening statement of the call, to memory.* A conversation (or even the prospect of a conversation) with an Approver can be stressful. If the call turns into a "what does my script say" exercise, you'll lock up, stress out, and sound awful. The Approver will disengage instantly. Accept that you must improvise. (I suggest you follow this advice with all four contacts, but it's particularly important to remember this advice during contacts with the hard-charging Approver.)

- *Internalize your message.* Don't concentrate on what your prospect Approver's response will be. Just speak from your gut, not your head.

- *Be authentic.* Don't try to be someone else. Be yourself. The attitude should be, "Yes, I'm a salesperson, and a darned good one."

- *Establish/reinforce your Equal Business Stature by presenting a balanced gain equation.* Balanced gain equations, you'll re-call, express the *entire* picture. They show the up side *and* any downside of your ideas. Some balanced gain equations may have no downside risk. Just the same, the equation must always be balanced. You *must not* sound like a robot reciting text, of course, but what you say could sound something like this: "*Sixty five of the Fortune 100* are increasing existing customer loyalty and add-on business by as much as 120 percent—while cutting direct sales expense by as much as 50 percent in just six months."

- *Never ask, "Did you get my letter?" or any variation thereof.* Approvers hate this. Others in the organization aren't likely to appreciate the implication that they're delinquent in opening, reading, or paying attention to their mail, either. If you sent a letter, simply repeat one of the points you raised in it, and let the Approver connect the dots.

- *Relate your expert industry knowledge.* Your products, services, and solutions can change this Approvers enterprise-wide per-formance. If they couldn't your organization would have a "going out of business" sign hanging in the window. Your first job is to relate relevant accomplishments and experience to this Approver. But don't drone on! Remember, you're operat-ing under an eight-second time limit. Identify the highlights of your company's best experiences with customers.

- *Provide a choice of several ideas.* The Approver, more than any other individual in the enterprise, requires choices. Approvers will often give commands such as: "Find me the top three producers of compressed air injection molds for our project

X—and do it fast!" So you're going to get used to saying something like this: "The ideas we have for your consideration consist of three performance areas. They are: increasing the size of every entry point order from new customers, cutting sales process time in half, and getting more high margin add-on business from existing customers. Which of these is important to you between now and let's say the end of this fiscal quarter?"

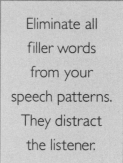

Eliminate all filler words from your speech patterns. They distract the listener.

- *Let the Approver interrupt you.* Expect it. If the call goes well, it will be because this person will be controlling it.

- *Near the end of your first conversation, suggest action items.* This applies to everyone you talk to on the phone; it's particularly important when talking to Approvers. The trick is, you have to do this in a way that allows the Approver to give the orders! What you say might sound something like this: "What would you like to see me and my team accomplish between now and the end of this business [week]?" Or: "Who on your team do you think I should be speaking with?" Once you've asked this question, listen up and take your marching orders!

- *Don't be afraid to do a reality check!* Approvers, you'll recall, hate wasting time. They also *respect* anyone who hates wasting time as much as they do! That means that you can and should ask the Approver a question you can't ask anyone else in the organization. It sounds something like this: "May I ask you for a personal favor?" (The Approver will say something like: "What's on your mind?") "Come the day when you approve the selection of the business partner that does X—[now mention the solution that you've been talking about]—whether it is or isn't my organization, would you grant me the privilege of an in-person meeting with you?" This gives you a second chance to sell—and perhaps pull the fat out of the fire—if something should go wrong later on in the sales cycle. Approvers almost always respond positively to this request. Give it a try.

- *Keep the door open.* Before you say goodbye, say something like this: "I'll keep you posted on my progress as I meet your other team members and uncover their needs."

On the Phone with the Decision Maker

When placing calls to these folks, always bear in mind that Decision Makers want to be treated as if *they were the Approver.* By treating the Decision Maker with the same business respect you would treat the Approver you'll be able to establish/reinforce your Equal Business Stature.

Here are some other guidelines for dealing with these all-important potential sponsors over the phone:

1. *Avoid stupid questions.* Don't say things like "Tell me a little about your business" or "What problems are you facing?" or "Are you interested in [cutting costs]?" You'll only insult the Decision Maker's intelligence.

2. *Focus on questions that let you identify this person's goals and reinforce the advantages of your ideas.* For instance: "What are the three most pressing issues facing you in the [accounting department's reporting capacities]?" "If you could change one performance parameter in your [production line] what would it be?" "Now that we're entering the [third fiscal quarter], what areas in your [shipping and receiving] department are you looking for with regards to [costs and efficiency]?"Stay focused on the results and how you tailor your products, services, and solutions to help achieve these goals.

3. *Connect this conversation (if possible) with something you learned over the phone from the Recommender.* For instance: "I've discovered from your [tool crib supervisor] that you're unintentionally replicating five steps during your [polishing] process. Three of my other process manufacturing customers are eliminating this excess by . . ."

> It's okay to say that you don't know, however, always offer to find out.

4. *Don't make any direct recommendations during the initial stages of the relationship.* That's sales malpractice, remember?

5. *End the conversation by suggesting an action item.* See the advice for calls with the Approver, above.

On the Phone with the Influencer

This is the player who likes salespeople least, and who will object most if you call on anyone else in the organization. My first piece of advice, then, is *not* to call these folks unless you absolutely have to or directed by an Approver or Decision Maker. Assuming that you *do* have to call this person, bear the following rules in mind:

1. *Emphasize your product knowledge.* This will help you establish or reinforce Equal Business Stature: You had best know your stuff when working with this player. So: No hedging, no fudging—just 100 percent correct facts and figures. If you don't know something, say so.
2. *Go easy on the success stories.* Influencers are not impressed with what you've done for others. They mostly care about what you can do for them.
3. *Connect this first conversation with whatever you did earlier.* If you took the time to prepare and send to the Influencer a detailed piece of correspondence, ask specific, quantifiable opinion questions about its technical content and validity. ("What was your opinion of the design criteria that our [test and development] engineers used to design our [Omega +5] synthesizer?")
4. *Don't press for a decision.* As we've discussed, you should stay away from terminology like "Are you prepared to . . ."
5. *Uncover an existing need that you can help satisfy.* The goal here is to uncover the need but don't let the Influencer know that you've uncovered it. It's best to let the Influencer take all of the credit for any uncovering of anything that remotely resembles a need, problem, or challenge. Whenever anyone asks (such as the Decision Maker or, Approver) whose idea addressed a problem, always give your Influencer the credit. (Remember, you're out to get a second appointment, and a commission check—not a pat on the back.)

6. *Tie any action items to the Influencer's ideas, projects, or desired results.* At the same time, you must maintain some kind of control over the time factor. Here's an example of what it might sound like:

YOU: When would you like for me to deliver the budgetary proposal you asked for?

INFLUENCER: I'll need that Friday.

YOU: Okay—that means my systems engineers need to get the configuration of your network by Tuesday. I can stop by at 8:15 on Tuesday to pick it up—or would you prefer to e-mail it to me?

On the Phone with the Recommender

If you start out your sales cycle as I've suggested (by contacting the Approver first), it's likely that he or she will point you toward a specific Recommender who can talk to you about the real-world implications of what you may eventually end up fixing for this company.

Here are some guidelines on effective phone contact with this player:

1. *Connect this call to whatever happened earlier.* The easiest way to do this is by saying, "I'm calling because Jim Bigshot [the Approver] thought that you'd be the best person for me to talk with." You now have the undivided attention of this person. (The same approach works well with Influencers and Decision Makers, but it has a way of making the Recommender feel like an instant celebrity, which is why I'm addressing it here.)

> Name dropping will win you Equal Business Stature if you use the right name!

2. *Focus on improvements.* Find out what the Recommender wants to better, finish faster, make easier, or make more rewarding. But remember—it's a fool's game to try to sell to this person. He or she has no authority and no approval

to buy anything. Explore by asking questions like, "*Would it be useful . . .*", "*Would you find it helpful . . .*", and "*What would happen if . . .*"

3. *Ask for "inside information."* No, not the kind that can get you in trouble with the Feds—just the stuff that the Recommender has access to and you don't. During or after the call, the Recommender can get you important background on who's who in the company. He or she can also help you track down non-confidential enterprise information such as bills, estimates, and procedure manuals, as well as copies of product literature, catalogs, annual reports, and the like. Again—if you've got the endorsement of the Approver, the Recommender will be highly motivated to get you whatever you need.

LOCK IN WHAT YOU'VE LEARNED

I invite you to participate in an e-learning exercise that I've developed based on this chapter. Visit www.gettingthesecondappointment .com and then click on Chapter 18 Online Assets. You'll get a chance to download several additional ideas for your first telephone conversation and other valuable information.

19

THE FIRST APPOINTMENT— TACTICAL APPROACHES

Getting an initial appointment is, of course, a prerequisite to getting the second appointment. In this chapter, I'll be giving you several different ways to set up the first meeting, all of which will build on the foundation strategies covered earlier in the book.

My goal is to give you a number of options, on the theory that some tactics will be more effective in your unique selling environment than others.

REALITY CHECK

Complete your TIP and identify your target prospect and his or her support team. You should know the Approver by name and title, a likely Decision Maker by name and title, Influencers by title, and Recommenders by title. You're ready to start working to secure your first appointment. (Ideally, you're going to reach out to the Approver to establish initial contact.)

Here's my short list of what I would most like to know *before* I contact an Approver:

- What's on the Approver's mind.
- What's on the Approver's calendar.
- What's on the Approver's "to-do" list.
- *What* does the Approver like and dislike.
- *Who* does the Approver like and dislike.
- What will the Approver read.
- Who will the Approver spend time with.
- The Approver's preferred mode of absorbing information.

> The Approver's personal assistant is a "know it all."

There is only one person (besides the Approver) who has the answers to all of these questions. That person is the Approver's personal assistant.

If you want to guarantee a successful first interaction with the Approver, make a call to the Approver's personal assistant. Most salespeople view any kind of interaction with these "gatekeepers" as something to be avoided or put off until absolutely necessary. These salespeople are concerned that the gatekeeper will reject them and not let them gain access to the Approver. However, remember that the Approver's personal assistant runs the show.

It is therefore important for you to get this person on your side. To do that, it helps to place a call; and to do that, it helps to know the person's name. To learn this, you can:

1. Call the receptionist.
2. Check the organization's web site for contact information.
3. Call the Approver's office directly.

My suggestion is that you try all three, in the order given, until you identify the name of the assistant. When you get to #3, of course, you will have to prepare for a number of outcomes:

1. The telephone will be picked up and a voice on the other end will say: "Ms. Importanta's office, how can I help you?" (You've reached the assistant!)

2. The telephone will be picked up and a voice on the other end will say: "Ms. Importanta." (You've reached the Approver!)
3. You hear a recorded message. (You've been dumped into voice mail jail!)

Whoever picks up the telephone at this point (don't worry, we'll get to voice mail in a moment), you have, for all intents and purposes, gotten the Approver on the line. In other words, if the Approver's personal assistant picks up the phone, you must forget every gatekeeper tactic you've ever learned. Forget the fact that you really would prefer to have a chat with the Approver. Forget *everything* except this simple rule: If you treat the personal assistant as if he or she were the Approver, one or more of the following things will take place:

1. You will build Equal Business Stature and Business Rapport with the assistant. (Not too bad.)
2. You will show that you appreciate and acknowledge his or her position of power. (This is better.)
3. You will be granted an appointment. (The best!)

WHAT TO SAY

This is the easy part. What we say must be fit for the ears of the Approver. Here's an example of what the dialogue might sound like:

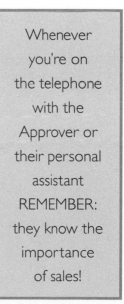

Whenever you're on the telephone with the Approver or their personal assistant REMEMBER: they know the importance of sales!

ASSISTANT: This is Tommie—how can I help you? (As soon as you hear the assistant's name, write it down!)

YOU: Tommie, this is Will Prosper with CoolCo—thanks for taking my call. We've never spoken before, but would you be willing to give me your opinion on an idea that [65 of the Fortune 100] find valuable? (Or: . . . on an idea that 25 other manufacturers here in San Diego find valuable? Or: . . . on an idea that [Important Person Whose Name Tommie May Recognize] finds valuable?)

Tommie will either say "Go ahead," or "What's this all about?" In either case, the spotlight is on you. What you say and how you say it will determine if you get the appointment.

Because you're at the Approver level, and you're treating Tommie as an Approver, what you say should be rich in benefits. For instance:

> YOU: We specialize in giving salespeople the tools they need to increase the size of each initial sale by as much as 54 percent while they compress their sales cycles up to 50 percent.

> TOMMIE: Well, Ms. Importanta is always on the lookout for ways to increase revenues while saving time.

> YOU: That's great news! What else is important to you?

> TOMMIE: Ms. Importanta is focused on improving our customer service ratings and brand recognition.

> YOU: Tommie, could you share with me your current ideas on how to do that?

> TOMMIE: Actually, Ms. Importanta is working with our business consultants right now, laying out our fourth quarter plan.

At this point, you can ask the assistant just about anything relating to the business . . . as long as you remember to treat him or her with same respect you would treat the Approver.

At the conclusion of this call, if you ask for help in setting up a meeting with the Approver, you will be very likely to get it. The assistant, after all (whom you've just turned into an ally), controls the Approver's calendar and what more important corporate resource is there than that?

DO YOU SEE WHAT'S HAPPENING HERE?

Every time you treat the assistant as a senior executive, you find out more about the Approver's priorities and strategies! It really works. Try it.

If, however, you were to succumb to force of habit and use one of those outdated gatekeeper tactics, you'd quickly find yourself on the outside looking in. For example:

You: Tommie, this is Will Prosper with CoolCo, thanks for taking my call. May I please speak with Ms. Importanta? (Big mistake! On this initial call, you must treat the assistant as the Approver—and you would never ask the Approver to put you in touch with "someone more important," especially not in the first five seconds of the conversation.)

Tommie: What's this in reference to? (If you'd asked Tommie's opinion on the initial exchange, you wouldn't be facing this dreaded question.)

You: It's about an idea [65 of the Fortune 100] find valuable that will be of interest to Ms. Importanta.

Tommie: Ms. Importanta is quite busy and has all the ideas she needs from her team of consultants. Thanks for the call. (Or: Ms. Important is quite busy; why don't you send some information and I'll pass it along to the appropriate person.) (Or: Our purchasing department handles all of these types of inquires. Hold on, let me connect you to the right person. You're put on hold . . . then you hear a raspy voice: Hi, this is Jimmy in purchasing; what's your vendor number?)

> Forget every single gatekeeper tactic you've ever learned!

You get the point. If you want to get an appointment with the "Big Cheese," make sure you treat the personal assistant as though he or she actually is the "Big Cheese."

WHAT IF THE APPROVER PICKS UP THE PHONE?

Don't be surprised if this happens. In my experience, 10 to 15 percent of the time when the phone rings on the assistant's desk the Approver picks it up. It doesn't happen often, but when it does, you'll be looking at an opportunity to schedule the first appointment and accelerate your sales cycle, so be ready for it.

Ms. Importanta: How can I help you?

You: Ms. Importanta, it's an honor to speak with you! This is Will Prosper with CoolCo. Would you be willing to give me your opinion on an idea that [65 of the Fortune 100] find valuable? (Or: "Ms. Importanta, it's an honor to speak with you! This is Will Prosper with CoolCo. 65 of the Fortune 100 are increasing the size of each new sale by as much as 54 percent while the cut their sales process time in half. Would you be interested in getting similar or even greater results before the end of this fiscal year?")

Stop talking. At this point, all you've got to do is follow the Approver's lead and make sure you've got your PDA or calendar handy. If there's an opportunity for a meeting, you'll know about it within the next 30 seconds or so, and the Approver will summon you in for an audience.

IF YOU GET DUMPED INTO VOICE MAIL

Treat voice mail like a person-to-person interaction. You'll get voice mail about 50 percent of the time. So don't be surprised or disappointed when this happens! You really don't need to remember any kind of script or special approach; just use the "bookend" approach, which employs an authentic and somewhat casual "intro" and "outro." For instance:

> *Tommie, if you were in your office to take my call this is what you would have heard: This is Will Prosper with CoolCo. Would you be willing to give me your opinion on an idea that [65 of the Fortune 100] find valuable that's proven to increase the size of every initial sale by as much as 54 percent while at the same time cutting sales process time in half? Call me, Will Prosper, any afternoon between 3 and 5 P.M. I look forward to hearing your response and understanding your level of interest. My number is (800) 777-8486. That's (800) 777-8486. Thanks for listening and have a great rest of the day!*

Say this at a moderate rate of speech, modulating your voice (and controlling everything else as per Chapter 18). A message like that should take you about 35 seconds to deliver.

THE SQUEEZE PLAY

This is an advanced first-appointment tactic I developed and continue to use to this day with great success. For it to work, you must be facing *all* of the following circumstances:

- The Approver and the Decision Maker must be located in the same geographical area or in the same office facility.
- You must know the name of one key individual who reports directly to the Decision Maker who will be an Influencer of your sale.

Here's how it works. First, prepare to send the Approver something of high value and interest. In my case, I send an autographed copy of one of my books with a page or two highlighted; you might choose to send an autographed copy of the most recent best-selling business book that mentions any metric that your product, service, or solution can affect positively. (Be sure to highlight that portion of the book that references this information. You can use a note or a nice bookmark.) Alternatively, you might send something "from the desk of" your CEO, president, or owner, such as a special invitation to meet the team. Whatever you choose to send the Approver, make sure it's something that he or she would want to show to the Decision Maker personally.

Next, prepare to send the key Influencer—who should, you'll recall, report directly to the Decision Maker—some kind of direct correspondence that is of high appeal. For example, in my case I'll send an area sales manager a CD that teaches a critical selling skill. Whatever *you* send the Influencer, make sure it's something he or she would want to show to the Decision Maker personally.

Send the Approver and the Influencer their items of interest on the same day by first-class mail.

On that day, pick up the telephone (after your prospect's hours of operation) and leave a voice mail message for the Decision Maker. Here's how my message sounds:

Phyllis, this is Tony Parinello the author of Selling to VITO, the Very Important Top Officer. *In the next few days, your*

CEO may ask you to take a look at my program that 65 of the Fortune 100 use. Your area sales manager may also mention my name to you. I'd love to chat with you at your earliest convenience. My schedule is open for the next three days between 3 P.M. and 5 P.M. My direct line is (800) 777-8486. Thanks for listening and have a great rest of the day.

Keep in mind that the purpose of this approach is to broadcast the awareness of what you do *one level above* and *one level below* your Decision Maker. Doing this will accelerate your sales process while at the same time build Equal Business Stature at all levels. It will also almost certainly land you a first appointment.

THE THIRD-PARTY INTRODUCTION

A more traditional method of securing a first appointment is through the use of a recognizable third party/person. There are only a two sources that I would recommend using:

1. The Approver or Decision Maker of an existing customer who is totally enamored with you and your value. (Note that Approvers tend to give referrals to other Approvers and Decision Makers tend to give referrals to other Decision Makers.)
2. A board member of your target prospect's company.

Let's start by looking at the first option. Imagine for a moment that you're sitting in the office of the Approver at your best customer. After you ensure that this Approver knows of the recent value you've been delivering lately and before you conclude your meeting, look at the Approver and say:

Margaret, may I ask a personal favor of you?

Stop talking. Wait until Margaret responds with something like:

Sure, what's on your mind?

Continue by saying:

Would you be willing to pick up your telephone and introduce me to a [president] that you personally know who may have a need for my services?

Now, wait until Margaret responds with something like: Let's see . . . I do know one or two people on my board who could use your help. Hold on, let me make a call.

You just hit first appointment "pay dirt"!

> Never hesitate to ask any Approver to call someone they know on your behalf.

How about board members? Here's how that strategy works. You take the time to get the names of each of a target prospect's board members. Then you take the time to find their telephone numbers. Then you actually place the call. The conversation goes something like this:

RECEPTIONIST: Acme, how may I direct your call?

YOU: This is Will Prosper, would you please connect me with Mr. Keyguy? Thank you.

RECEPTIONIST: May I tell him what the call is about?

YOU: Yes, please tell him it's about BeaconCorp—the organization he is a board member of. Thanks for putting my call through.

After a short pause you hear a voice on the other end of the line: "Ima Keyguy."

YOU: Mr. Keyguy, thanks for taking my call. My name is Will Prosper with IdeaCo, we've never met but I have a proven idea that could [create additional revenue while at the same time cutting expenses within the next fiscal quarter] for [Beacon-Corp]. Can I bounce the idea off you?

KEYGUY: Sure, what's it about?

Now you speak casually, laying your ideas out in a fashion that this high-level person can understand. (In other words, you focus on benefits and advantages.) At the end of your dialogue with this all-important player, you say:

In your opinion what's the best way to bring this to the attention of Ms. Importanta (now, mention the name of the Approver at your target enterprise)?

ss what? If you did your job in laying out your value, the
member will usually say: "Let me give her a call right now.
's your number? I'll call you right back."

The reason that board members will usually take your idea to
the top themselves is simple: They want to serve the best interests
of the organization whose board they sit on. They want to be a
part of its success; they want to be *useful,* which means having
their ideas used. They also get acknowledged at the next board
meeting. They also benefit financially from the increase in shareholder value . . . not bad!

Proof positive (as though you needed it) that referral selling is
the only way to sell.

"TACTICAL AIR SUPPORT" FROM YOUR CEO, PRESIDENT, OR OWNER

By my estimate, two-thirds of all CEOs, presidents, and owners of
organizations today were once salespeople. They made cold calls,
probed for needs, made presentations, went for the "close," won
deals and, yes, lost deals to the competition. The other one-third
of this population has, at the very least, a profound appreciation of
the importance of what you and I do for a living. (CEOs who don't
appreciate the importance of salesforces tend not to stay CEOs for
very long.)

As a general rule, all these top people are eager to engage in
some way, shape, or form in the sales process. Now, I don't suggest
that an entire salesforce of thousands of salespeople can ask their
top officers to make initial sales calls for them. I do, however, want
you to understand that your company's top officer
is almost certainly willing to pick up the telephone
and make a call for you if doing so will help you
move a significant opportunity forward.

> I've yet to meet a successful Approver that hesitates to make a sales call.

Find the five or ten largest potential prospects in
your territory—the ones with the most recognizable brands and logos. Create a list that shows the
names and telephone numbers of the Approvers
and their assistants at each of these organizations.
Alongside each name place your estimate of this

TABLE 19.1   Approvers and their assistants.

Name	Assistant	Telephone	Estimated Lifetime Value ($ in Millions)
Leslie Allen	Jere	(619) 815-7652	3.8
Kathleen Brooks	Julie	(858) 748-0932	2.9
Steven Keyes	James	(760) 876-9989	1.2
Caroline Brewer	Erica	(890) 444-5500	4.5

person's potential lifetime value to your organization. Your list could look something like Table 19.1.

You get the picture—and so will your top officer. Assuming you do the "heavy lifting" up front by compiling the list, creating the correspondence, and so on, there isn't a CEO, president, or owner who wouldn't pick up the phone and make a call of introduction to such a list of contacts.

When I describe this strategy to salespeople, they sometimes laugh nervously. Believe me when I tell you that this is *no joke*. All you really need to do is prepare your "hit list" of potential prospects, show this book to your Top Officer with this chapter highlighted, and stand back. You're about to be booked into a wave of initial meetings with the most important Approvers in your territory. Cha Ching!

LOCK IN WHAT YOU'VE LEARNED

I invite you to participate in an e-learning exercise that I've developed based on this chapter. Visit www.gettingthesecondappointment .com and then click on Chapter 19 Online Assets. You'll get a chance to participate in an e-lesson and download other valuable information.

20

ACTION ITEMS— WINDOWS TO THE SECOND APPOINTMENT

Have you ever experienced an inexplicable loss of momentum in a sales situation?

In other words, have you ever gotten caught up in the excitement of being with a prospect whom you thought was a perfect fit—someone who seemed to have the perfect set of needs for what you were selling, but who for some odd reason *didn't* end up buying from you, or even participating in future discussions?

We can reduce the likelihood of this common problem by getting very clear on what exactly we want the prospect to do at the end of the first appointment. Yes, you do have the right—and, I would argue, the responsibility—to ask the prospect to take on specific action items at the conclusion of the first meeting. Choosing the *right* action for the *right* person is extremely important.

Here's a summary of what, specifically, you should be willing to ask each of the four key players to take action on at the conclusion of the first meeting. In the ideal case, each of these action items should be used as a tool to get you closer to a scheduled *second* meeting with the Approver and/or Decision Maker and making the sale in two calls.

ACTION ITEMS FOR RECOMMENDERS

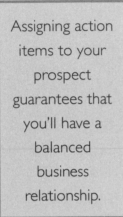

Assigning action items to your prospect guarantees that you'll have a balanced business relationship.

The best "homework" to give your Recommenders will be for them to gather up information about any steps in their daily activities that they are currently taking unnecessarily.

Ask Recommenders to dream about the perfect process in the perfect world. Ask them to brainstorm about what they could do differently. If there were no limits, what would make their job easier, faster, better, more rewarding, and more satisfying? Of course, all of this should be related to the area of expertise that you could help them with. What the Recommender eventually comes up with may help you in later discussions with Approvers and Decision Makers.

Remember: Asking the Recommender to take responsibility for advancing the sale for you is a huge strategic error that will cost you time, effort, and energy.

ACTION ITEMS FOR INFLUENCERS

Ask these people for data, whether it comes in the form of training manuals, systems configuration specifications, telephone bills, flow charts, or anything else that describes the current situation and/or the products, services, and solutions the organization happens to be using right now.

You might ask Influencers to provide you with a written list or matrix of their current evaluation criteria. You might ask them to provide information on how they will be evaluating or testing whatever it is you happen to be selling. Whatever you ask for, be prepared to get it in writing . . . and be prepared for detail. You can use all that detail to support later discussions with Approvers and/or Decision Makers.

Don't ask an Influencer to help you redesign your current product or service offering!

ACTION ITEMS FOR DECISION MAKERS

Don't be shy about proposing action items for Decision Makers or Approvers. The higher up you go in the hierarchy of any organization, the more understanding your contacts will be about taking on an appropriate action item and being held accountable for it.

Your action items for the Decision Maker should center on higher level initiatives that affect the decision-making process within the organization. Ask these people for help in identifying policies, practices, and procedures; formal and informal networks of authority; terms and conditions of doing business; and any compliance issues that the company's business partners are required to conform to.

Consider initiating a dialogue along the following lines at the end of your first meeting with the Decision Maker.

YOU: My organization is getting ready to spend a fair amount of presales resources to work with your team. I take this responsibility seriously so, if it's okay with you, I'd like to ask you to do me a personal favor.

DECISION MAKER: What's on your mind?

YOU: Would you please put together a list of your expectations and requirements for selecting a provider of solutions that can help you [secure your performance and compliance requirements] in the area of _____? (Fill in this blank with your area of expertise.) You could e-mail this to me or I could stop by and pick it up.

ACTION ITEMS FOR APPROVERS

Your action items for the Approver should center on the business-to-business aspects of your future relationship. You should ask this person for help in developing a quantifiable list that you can share

> You'll gain *Equal Business Stature* points whenever you ask an Approver to take on an action item.

with your CEO, president, or owner about what this particular Approver looks for from his or her business partners. The Approver can help you obtain and/or exchange annual reports or any other appropriate financial documents.

Most Approvers know that your organization may require credit references for new relationships. Don't gloss over these requirements or make light of them. Approvers make the same request of their own prospects. So when they hear you making this request, they will applaud your due diligence and personal accountability.

Keep your business relationship in balance by asking the Approver to take responsibility for answering a critical question whose answer will reflect the real-world likelihood of your doing business together. Ask your contact: *"If you were in my shoes, would you feel comfortable authorizing in the neighborhood of [$XX,000] in presales resources to support this relationship?"* The number in brackets is the number that you must have a grip on. Do you know how much it costs your company, in terms of time and resource allocation, to launch a new business relationship? If the answer is "no," stop here and make your best estimate of what it typically costs your organization to sell whatever it is you're selling to a single new prospect. Once you have the answer, you'll be prepared to ask every Approver in your prospective account base this all-important "if you were in my shoes" question. Even if you feel uncomfortable at first, ask the question near the close of the first meeting. (If the answer turns out to be "no," don't you think you and your sales manager deserve that information up front?)

By the way, if you ever need an excuse to assign an action item to any Approver, you can say something along the following lines: "My CEO has asked me to get some specific information from every leader of every organization that is considering our products, services, and solutions. Would you help me in fulfilling her request?"

PRACTICE MAKES PATIENCE

There is no doubt that learning to ask for the "right stuff" at the end of the first appointment will all but guarantee your second appointment.

Let's head for the barn . . . turn to the last chapter of the book!

FROM COACH STEVE

CRITICAL SALES SUCCESS STEPS—STEP 6:
CONSTRUCT A STRUCTURE OF SUPPORT AND
ACCOUNTABILITY

We are wrapping up a terrific journey, and redefining your potential for success in selling. If you have followed the coaching plan laid out in our chats, then you are in a great position to make Tony's program pay off for you . . . and you've roughed out a powerful plan for reaching the levels of success you know you are capable of.

In this, the final step in the six Critical Sales Success Steps, I will encourage you construct a Structure of Support and Accountability.

If we were to meet personally, and you told me all of the plans you have in mind for implementing the ideas and insights you have gained by reading this book, I would be interested and you would have high hopes. After a few weeks went by, if you are like most every human being on the planet, your ideals would have faded and most if not all of your plan would have evaporated into the day-to-day routine of obligations, challenges, and competing time demands. You would have already rationalized that you would "get to it all later when you have time to think" and another sales quarter would pass—then two and finally a whole year would pass by. Your sales performance would be a bit better but you would be in the bookstore looking for another version of the "secret sauce."

(continued)

But what if, after you told me all about your plans to implement all these ideas and detailed for me your action plan (Step 5 at the end of Chapter 17), I turned to you and said, "That's terrific! How about you and I meet back here in a couple of weeks so that you can tell me what you have accomplished, specifically? Then we could tweak the plan and chart out next steps."

Do you think you would have more done in two or three weeks? How about the sales quarter? And what would the sales year look like if we kept that up?

We all need accountability and support. You need cheerleaders and encouragers around you who believe in you. You need advisors to help you answer questions and lead you to more information as you grow. And you need coaches—at least one—to help you navigate the journey and champion your continued focus.

Make a list of all the people who can fulfill roles on your "Super Success Support Team." Include all the individuals that you can invite to provide a cushion around you that fear, inconsistency, doubts, and obstacles cannot penetrate. Build an army of support that will lift you up and beyond your ideals for realizing your potential. Include:

➢ Your boss or manager.
➢ Coworkers you trust and can confide in.
➢ Your Spouse.
➢ Nonselling peers who believe in you.
➢ Administrative assistants or support team members who you can enroll in your goals.
➢ Executives from other companies who can advise you.
➢ Other successful sales professionals in other companies or markets.
➢ Friends who believe in you.
➢ A professional coach (see www.gettingthesecondappointment .com for suggestions).
➢ "Virtual" coaches and trainers such as Tony and other success gurus.

Finally, be sure to build your own *personal accountability system*. Make sure that you keep in front of you the materials that you have worked on throughout this book. Bookmark www.gettingthesecondappointment.com. Enroll in the SuccessPortal program offered by Tony. Use a whiteboard or other visuals to track your success. Generally saturate your environment with tools, reminders, and resources that support your awareness and focus for sales success.

Now finish Tony's book . . . and get to work!

21

THE 10 POWERS

Most books end with short chapters, because authors have pretty much said it all by this point and are interested in wrapping everything up. This book is different.

The final chapter is not a short one, and for good reason. This, as it happens, is where the most critical information in the entire book appears.

What you're about to read is information that is probably *not* going to be of much use to you if you're flipping through the book and arrived at the last chapter by accident. This is not because I want to make your life difficult, but because everything that shows up here demands a familiarity with all the information that's gone before.

If you've mastered the principles in the previous 20 chapters, you're ready to use the 10 most powerful selling steps there are. When used properly, these tactics will create a chain-reaction that *will* result in your either making the sale in two calls—or identifying, *early on in the sales cycle,* a contact you're not going to sell to right now. (If you stop to think how much time most salespeople spend interacting with people who have no interest whatsoever in buying, you'll realize that's actually a pretty important piece of information.)

Warning: Please do not skip any step, modify any step, or change the order of anything that appears in this chapter!

ARE YOU READY?

Just a few words of preparation are in order, so please bear with me while I share them with you.

You must approach the 10 power steps with confidence, not skepticism. The biggest question I get from salespeople when I talk about these power steps is, "Can I *really* expect to close the sale by the second face-to-face appointment?" My answer is "Yes—at the very least you can certainly close *more* business along this time line than you're currently closing. Your state of mind is vitally important in implementing the power steps."

During my radio talk show "Selling Across America" (www .sellingacrossamerica.com), a salesperson named Larry is a regular caller. Larry sells A.C. power conditioning equipment to industrial customers.

Here's his first story. Larry made his initial call into a qualified prospective account six months ago at the Influencer level and found himself totally pigeonholed, blocked, stymied, and stalled. You could hear the frustration in his voice. He was racking up his cost of sales while the chances of his getting the deal diminished with each passing day. I gave Larry the same advice you're about to read.

Later on, my audience heard Larry's second story. This time, Larry sounded supremely confident. He had made a call to a qualified account at the Approver level. In this case, however, he consummated the deal in *just two meetings*.

How did he do it? Well, Larry used some simple tactics that I've perfected over the years; tactics that have the potential for making the two-call close a reality for you, too—if you're willing to follow a few *simple* rules, and discard a few *complex* rules.

Let me explain what exactly I mean by *simple* and *complex*. Just about any sale can be classified as simple or complex. The label applies to the sales process itself, not what is being sold, and whether or not you face a simple or a complex sales cycle will *definitely* affect your strategies for securing a first, second, or subsequent appointment—and for making the sale.

Let's take a quick look now at both selling situations. Let's look at a complex sale first.

Traditionally, a complex sale is a sale that involves several (i.e., more than two), individuals who play the role of a Recommender and are asked to evaluate purchasing options. This kind of sale may, for instance, include a committee of "users" with varying backgrounds, interests, and capabilities. In the complex sale, you're also likely to face several people who will play the all-important role of Influencer, not just one or two. (There's a good chance that you'll encounter consultants who play this role in the complex sale at some point in your sales career.)

All those Influencers will, most likely, require an ocean of analysis and evaluation, and maybe a few demonstrations thrown in for good measure. Then there are, in the complex sale, usually customer sites, referrals, and perhaps a factory or facilities tour thrown in for good measure. Of course, you'll have the typical Decision Maker and the Approver to deal with; to make things a bit more interesting, in the complex sale, it's possible that those people may not be in the same geographic location as the Recommenders and Influencers you meet.

> We need to blend the revenue potential of a complex sale with the timing of a simple sale.

In the complex sale, you generally find approval cycles that are longer than the grocery store checkout line on Friday at around 5:00 P.M.

If you're selling office supplies (a fairly simple product) and you happen to be working on a large account with many needs and more than one location, you can bet your last paper clip that you're in a complex sale. Bottom line: Many salespeople who sell "simple" stuff (paper, furniture, tongue depressors) end up doing so in *extremely* complex sales cycles.

Typically, a complex sale has with it the potential of add-on orders after the initial sale: purchase options, consumables, service contracts, and the like. This type of opportunity can create a somewhat "passive" revenue stream and an annuity for commissioned salespeople.

The simple sale, by contrast, is one that has quick evaluations and decision cycles that typically take place on the first or second sales call. Salespeople tend to like these sales a lot more than the other variety of sale but the truth is that the average dollar value in the sales cycle be demonstrably lower than in the complex sale.

In the simple sale, the Recommender and the Influencer may well be one and the same person! From time to time, you'll come across this "doubling-up" phenomenon in this simple kind of sale. In fact, my favorite simple sale is the one where *all* of the players are one person. It's so easy to figure out where you stand!

Then there are the simple sales where the Decision Maker and the Approver sit in adjacent offices . . . or are related . . . or both. Now *that's* a hierarchical structure that can get you a definitive answer in a hurry.

Of course, your product, service, or solution does not have to be either simple or inexpensive to fit into this category. For example, if you're selling those huge 18-wheeler auto-transporters to the owner of a small trucking company, that $300,000 rig you're showing off may be complex—but the sales process is simple, because in all likelihood you're only dealing with one person. Want it, need it, see it, like it, buy it! (Wow, that was quick!) But if you were to take the exact same product and try to sell it to a nationally known, multiple-location transportation firm, you'd find *yourself* transported into the wonderful world of the complex sale.

My job in this chapter is to give you the tools you need to keep each and every complex sale as robust as Nature meant it to be . . . while at the same time allowing the complex sale to take on the look and feel of the simple sale's process!

Do me a favor right now by reading the following statements aloud:

- I would like my sales process to be shorter.
- I would like my average sale to be bigger.
- I want *all* of the hard-earned, add-on business I deserve from my existing customers.

- I want to spend less time jumping through hoops with getting the sale.

How many of the statements you just read do you actually agr with? If you're like every other salesperson in America, you agree with each of the items.

Here's my point: You can come closer to each of these worthy objectives by helping to make your *complex* sales process a little more like the *simple* sales process . . . and, in the process, have more time, more money, and more fun.

The truth is, complex sales are usually made *more* complex by the actions salespeople take. It's my strong belief that we can make the typically lengthy, complex sale shorter and simpler—and do a much better job of setting up second and subsequent appointments in both selling environments—just by changing a few simple actions that most of us have been conditioned to take over the years. I'm talking about rectifying fundamental selling errors and replacing them with practical, tactical tips for making the sale . . . often, in two calls.

So here, without further ado, are the 10 Power Steps.

THE 10 POWER STEPS

Here are the 10 power steps you must take in this order to either (1) quickly determine that you don't have a match with the company you're targeting or (2) close the sale in two calls. In this chapter, I'm going to challenge you to take advantage of:

1. The power of starting at the top.
2. The power of your terms and conditions.
3. The power of familiarity.
4. The power of urgency.
5. The power of curiosity.
6. The power of touch.
7. The power of objections.
8. The power of satisfaction.
9. The power of greed.
10. The power of the customer.

Let's look at each of these steps right now.

Step One—The Power of Starting at the Top

If the Approver of your own organization were going to launch a sales process to sell your product, service, or solution to a qualified prospect that fit your TIP, whom do you think he or she would reach out too first—the Recommender, the Influencer, the Decision Maker, or the Approver?

Of course: the Approver. Therefore, *you* must act like the Approver and *always* make your own first call on the Approver. No ifs, ands, or buts.

As you find yourself creating the correspondence, picking up the telephone, or walking into the office of the Approver for the first time, ask yourself: If *my* Approver was doing this, what would she/he be doing? If you're in doubt, visit or call your organization's Approver. Let *him or her* coach you. If for some reason your organization's Approver can't be recruited, then go to your best existing customer and seek guidance.

If you don't follow this step—the other nine *will not work!*

Step Two—The Power of Your Terms and Conditions

As I've mentioned, we salespeople always wait too long to present our terms and conditions. If you want to make sure your sale stalls at the very moment you want it to accelerate, then you should present your terms and conditions at or near the end of your sales cycle.

> If title to title were really the rule by which the business world operated, nobody would sell much of anything!

If, on the other hand, you wish to accelerate the cycle, you should share your standard terms and conditions *with the Approver at the conclusion of the first meeting,* (more on this in just a moment).

Yes, you really do have to get in the habit of bringing your typical terms and conditions contract or other documentation on your first appointment. Waiting any longer is just too risky. After all:

- The longer we wait the more we've got invested in the deal in terms of time, presales resources, and opportunity cost (i.e., while we've been working on this deal we may not be paying as much attention as we should to other deals).

- If we wait until late in the relationship to discuss our terms and conditions, then we are deliberately choosing the point in the relationship when we have the least power if there are any negotiations to be made. That's not a good thing.
- Once presented, our terms and conditions may have to be reviewed by company attorneys whose job it is to "find something wrong"! That takes time. That extra time tagged on to your sales cycle may be just what your competition needs to make some substantial progress to stealing the deal from right under your nose.
- There may well be a deal-breaker in your standard terms and conditions. Don't you want to know about that up front?

Before you set out for your first appointment with any Approver, make sure you've got a fresh copy of your company's standard terms and conditions of the sale in your briefcase. At the end of your first appointment, just as you're walking out the door, reach into your briefcase and pull out the documentation and say something that's close to: "Ms. Importanta, here's my organization's standard terms and conditions of the sale. I've highlighted areas that we need to finalize such as the list of [equipment], [lease or purchase], and [service terms], however, the balance of the document is quite complete. Could you please let me know if there is anything in this document that you may not want to agree to should you decide to invest in our [products, services, or solutions]?"

Caution: Using this approach with any Influencer will almost certainly kill your sale. Again: Don't change any of the power steps.

Step Three—The Power of Familiarity

Help your prospect's Approver become familiar with you and your organization before, during, and after meeting you.

Marketing research tells us that if a person sees and/or experiences a product or idea or anything else for that matter seven times they are then familiar with that item or concept. In prior chapters, we spoke about sending correspondence—letters, faxes, e-presentations, and the like. What I'd like to suggest here is that you create a wave of familiarity around you and your products, services, and solutions.

Your organization would have to spend many millions of dollars to establish that kind of brand awareness for every Approver in your sales territory. But you can pull it off at a mere fraction of that cost. I've always felt that it is the job of the salesperson to do this kind of "local" brand awareness campaign. The following sequence of events can help you establish the prospect Approver's familiarity with you and your company.

You should create a "wave" of no less than seven pieces of correspondence that you'll send your prospect as the relationship unfolds. These can include but need not be limited to:

1. A letter of introduction of your ideas and value (real or suspected, hard or soft) and/or announcement of an accomplishment in your prospect's niche/industry. (Then you make a phone call.)
2. An e-mail of a suggested agenda and the date and time of the first appointment. (Then you make a phone call.)
3. A confirmation of the first appointment date, time, and location. (Then you actually have the first appointment with the Approver. Follow with:)
4. A thank-you note after the first appointment.
5. A note confirming the action items from the first appointment (similar to your GAP analysis). (You may want to follow this with a phone call to make sure all of it is agreed on.)
6. An e-mail of a suggested agenda for the second appointment. (Then you make a phone call to confirm these points.)
7. A confirmation of the second appointment date, time, and location.

Now that's familiarity! (See the online assets for this chapter for some sample letters, e-mails, thank-you notes, and first-call monologs.)

Step Four—The Power of Urgency

For Approvers and Decision Makers, the element of time is deeply interwoven with every reward and every fear. Time is *the* critical factor. You must clearly articulate how time intensifies the feeling of a specific reward or a specific fear.

Before you show up for your first appointment, calculate your estimate of the *total potential value* of your products, services, and solutions to your prospect. Once you have completed this task, you need only find out *what* this prospect is motivated by—reward or fear—and *when* they must take action to achieve a specific reward or avoid a specific fear. You can accomplish this by asking a question along these lines:

"Mr. Big Shot, what's personally important to you about [moving your operations to southern Florida] between [now] and the [end of this fiscal year]?"

Notice the use of the word *personally,* which tells you the "what," and the incorporation of *time* which will give you an idea of the "when."

If you hear: "If I don't, the cost of union labor here in New Jersey will drive me out of business."

Mr. Big is making an attempt to avoid "Fear." Position your solution as the antidote to this fear, and what you propose will be perceived as urgently important.

If you hear:

"Being located in southern Florida will put me closer to my Central American marketplace and keep me a step ahead of my competition."

> Not every Approver will respond to a benefit... some will look closer at the consequences of not having it.

In this case, Mr. Big is making an attempt to obtain a Reward. Position your solution as the means to this reward, and what you propose will be perceived as urgently important.

Step Five—The Power of Curiosity

Do everything you can to raise the level of your Approver's curiosity in your correspondence, over the telephone or during face-to-face meetings.

In your correspondence, use phrases like:

"There's much more to discuss that I would prefer to go over in person."
("What is it you want to tell me in person?")

"We were able to deliver an X percent increase in sales for ABC Company . . . while reducing their marketing expenses."

("How the heck did you pull that off?")

During a telephone conversation, mention right up front that before the end of the call you'll want to disclose an important benefit to this Approver for the accomplishment of a certain goal, plan, or objective.

("Please remind me to cover . . ." or "Before we end our call, we'll talk about . . .")

In person, during your first appointment with your Approver, use something very similar to the phrases that follow:

- "In just a moment, we can explore what [65 of the Fortune 100] . . ."
- "Before too long, let's make sure we talk about . . ."

Step Six—The Power of Touch

This one's pretty simple. The sooner you get your prospect Approver to touch, see, or feel your product, service, or solution, the more likely you are to make the sale in two calls. Move from the abstract to the specific. Get the Approver involved in a live demonstration or trial of whatever it is you offer. If possible, do this on the first meeting.

If you sell information or services, you may want consider making a prefirst meeting online demonstration using a company called "Brainshark" (www.brainshark.com). Brainshark offers a superb web-based, e-presentation tool.

Step Seven—The Power of Objections

The flip side of objection handling (which we've all been taught how to do) is *objection raising*—identifying the most likely obstacle to the sale and raising it yourself as a topic of discussion. As it turns out, this strategy is even more powerful than objection handling and you don't need to have much experience to pull it off.

No matter how good your products, services, and solutions are they are bound to have shortcomings in the eyes of some if not all of your prospects. Knowing this and bringing up the objection yourself *before* the Approver of your sale does so can be a very powerful strategy. Doing this can disarm your prospect and reduce the impact of the pending objection on your sales efforts. Objection raising builds credibility for you and your organization—while keeping you in the driver's seat of the appointment and sale.

If you don't raise a *real* objection, this sales tactic can backfire, causing your prospect to think that you're trying to cover-up something that's more substantial. How will you know what objection to raise? If you have any doubt, you can poll your peers, your service technicians, your manager—or ask your best customers in the industry of the prospect you're calling on.

> It's more powerful for you to raise an objection than for your prospect to raise it.

At or near the end of your first appointment, you can make a statement to your Approver similar to:

> "Mr. Big, there is one other point that is important for you to know. You may find that the overall [cost of ownership] our [web-based marketing system] to be somewhere in the neighborhood of [15 percent] higher than anyone else in this market. There's a good reason for this. Our ability to [create additional revenue] for your organization is [50 percent] greater than your current efforts and your [knowledge based] workers will enjoy greater [efficiency] due to our ease of use and [customer service help desk]."

There. All the cards are on the table. Either you will build a partnership with this person in spite of the cost factor . . . or you won't. (My bet is that you will.)

Take a deep breath and try it during the first appointment. It works.

Step Eight—The Power of Satisfaction

This step is all about identifying and broadcasting the right guarantee.

Whenever your prospect Approver reads or hears your guarantee and/or commitment to customer satisfaction, he or she should think or say out loud, "Man, they must really believe in their product" or, "Gee, how can they do that?" or, "Wow—they're really going to get ripped off by people taking advantage of them!"

If your Approvers typically have these kinds of reactions, then you may rest assured that you've got a satisfaction proposition that supports you in your effort to win the second appointment and close the sale within two visits. Your guarantee must startle your prospect a little—and then put his or her mind at ease. For a service such as kitchen remodeling, it should sound something like this:

"We guarantee our workmanship." (weak)

"We guarantee our workmanship and we'll finish your remodel on time." (not much better)

"We guarantee our workmanship and we'll finish your remodel in four weeks." (better)

"We guarantee our workmanship for as long as you own your home and we'll finish your remodel in four weeks. If we don't we'll pay you $200.00 for each day we're late." (best)

Believe it or not, having a guarantee that has a time limit on it—like "get a full refund if you're not satisfied in 30 days"—can actually work against you. The prospect will feel like he or she is under the gun to use (and perhaps abuse) your product within that time period, and to uncover any of its faults.

Take a moment right now and write out a guarantee for your product, service, and/or solution that will elicit the response we spoke about a minute ago. Do this even if you don't have the power to implement the solution; then bounce it off the right people within your organization. (Show them this chapter; they'll probably appreciate your initiative, understand what you're trying to accomplish, and give you the okay—especially if you're dealing with your top management.)

Step Nine—The Power of Greed

Greed is a powerful motivator.

No one likes to lose out. Most human beings want to get *more* than they paid for. They want something extra, something of *value*. This is especially true of Approvers.

Here's how you must put this reliable principle of human nature to work for your sale. (No, I'm not about to tell you to slash your price.)

Over the past several years, I've personally trained over one million salespeople. At least 85 percent of them provide consulting services for free—*and* about 60 percent of the prospects they are consulting with will never buy from them! That's a pile of free consulting that someone other than the prospect is paying for.

Add a line item or two to your proposals, invoices, RFPs (Requests for Proposals), RFIs (Requests for Information), and RFQs (Request for Quotations) that list the hourly fee for your presale consultative selling services. Then add an explanation *that the fee shown will be waived if the prospect purchases your products, services, and/or solutions within a certain period of time.*

Make sure that the Terms and Conditions you'll be showing the Approver include the explanation of the consulting services you'll be providing. I often highlight them in yellow.

Step Ten—The Power of the Customer

It's easier to get a customer to buy from you than it is to get a prospect to buy that same item.

We must, as suggested elsewhere in this book, make it extremely easy for prospects to become customers. I am not suggesting that we remove our requirements for trade references or cut our price by 75 percent. What I am suggesting, though, is that we move from the complex to the simple sales model in practice and in theory, no matter what it is you happen to be selling: computer chips or potato chips.

A happy customer is the most effective sales tool you have.

In this last power step, I'm challenging you to reposition your product offering. Engage your prospective Approver to move forward with a "thin slice" of your ideas (and the money it takes to invest in them).

In other words, solve the immediate problem now. Scale down your implementation time frames . . . and you'll get your prospects to turn into customers as quickly and as painlessly as possible. Then you won't be dealing with a prospect. You'll be dealing with a customer who's back for some high-margin, add-on business.

LOCK IN WHAT YOU'VE LEARNED

I invite you to participate in an e-learning exercise that I've developed based on this chapter. Visit www.gettingthesecondappointment .com and then click on Chapter 21 Online Assets. You'll get a chance to download many examples of the 10 Power Tips and various other worthwhile information.

CONGRATULATIONS!

You have reached the Starting Line! One that has great promises of tomorrow and many months and years to come of over quota performance and commission checks that are big enough to buy you anything you deserve.

What are you waiting for? Start running!

INDEX

A Special Offer

Your investment in this book entitles you to access four critical assets to enhance your success in sales:

1. *On-line collateral:* Several chapters of this book refer to additional information, charts, forms, and e-learning lessons on the World Wide Web. To access this information, go to: www.gettingthesecondappointment.com.
2. *On-line coaching:* Research shows that if you took two individuals with equal skill, motivation, and opportunity, the one with a personal success coach will always outperform the one who acts on his or her own. As you access the on-line assets, I invite you to participate in my one-of-a-kind Sales Success Portal.
3. *Weekly mentoring:* I host an Internet talk-show that's dedicated to salespeople and their continued success. I have other best selling authors, sales trainers, and best-practices experts join me. Go to: www.sellingacrossamerica.com for the show schedule.
4. *Seminars and keynote speeches:* Anthony Parinello is one of the nation's top sales trainers and motivational speakers. To inquire about his speaking schedule, availability, and fees, visit his web site or call his office: www.sellingtoVITO.com [800-777-VITO (8486)]

It's time to turn Thinking and Dreaming into Action and Living!

—Anthony Parinello